YOUR HOME REVEALS EVERYTHING ABOUT YOU

Aur
&
Vickghy Umythy

Your Home Reveals Everything is for entertainment and educational use only. In no way do the authors herein guarantee any results from applying the information within this material.

2017 Paperback Edition

Copyright © 2017 by Vickghy Umythy

All rights reserved.

Published in Thailand by Vickghy Umythy.

No part of this publication may be reproduced, distributed, or transmitted in any form or by any means, including photocopying, recording, or other electronic or mechanical methods, without the prior written permission of the publisher, except in the case of brief quotations embodied in critical reviews and certain other noncommercial uses permitted by copyright law.

For permission requests, email the author, addressed "Attention: Permissions" at the address below.

info@askaur.com
www.askaur.com

Ordering Information:
Quantity sales. Special discounts are available on bulk purchases by corporations, associations, and others. For details, contact the author at the address above.

Available for download from www.askaur.com
Available from February 2017 on Amazon.com in print and Kindle formats.

Illustrations by Tanasurn Thamsuriya

"We're not separate from the world around us. Our health, relationships, finances, and even sex lives are all influenced by our natural and man-made surroundings. Using this connection, we're able to transform our lives.

This book reveals that connection."

Vickghy Umythy

Preface

YOUR HOME REVEALS EVERYTHING is a collection of lessons and practical advice gathered by Vickghy (Vick) while studying alongside his mentor Aur in Bangkok, Thailand.

Aur is one of the world's foremost Feng Shui experts and resides in Bangkok, Thailand. Over the last 20 years, Aur has consulted for over five billion dollars' worth of property and has advised over 200 of Asia's wealthiest individuals, corporations, and politicians.

Between 2003 to 2011, Aur was also the host of a self-titled national TV show in Thailand which showcased her as she provided in-house consultations for fans all over Thailand. Nowadays Aur spends her time mentoring a handful of students and sharing her unique knowledge and wisdom both online and in the classroom.

In this book, we focus on the distinct connection between our daily lives and our physical surroundings (namely, our home). We cover how concepts such as the classical elements and the universal dichotomous forces of masculinity and femininity directly influence all areas of our lives. Everything from how we spend money to our private sex lives can be explained using these two. Everything in this book can be described as Feng Shui, linking the natural world to human experience. But it's important not to compare what you read in this book to any of the widely known Traditional Chinese schools of Feng Shui. The styles herein are unique to Aur and differ significantly from commonly held Feng Shui beliefs. In fact, we often directly challenge and contradict popular Feng Shui concepts.

We want you, the reader, to test everything in this book for yourself. There is nothing in here that asks for blind acceptance or that requires belief for it to be relevant to your life. We don't discuss chi, luck, or other esoteric ambiguity. Our purpose for this book is to share relevant and useful knowledge, as simply as possible.

In contrast to what is most commonly said, please do try everything you see here at home. We want you to use what you learn in this book to understand how your surroundings influence your life, and how to use this connection to your advantage in life.

We hope you enjoy the knowledge and resources provided in this book and utilize it as a tool in your journey of self-inquiry and development.

Vickghy Umythy

Contents

Preface v
Introduction 1

Chapter 1
Connecting History 3

Chapter 2
Fundamentals 10

Chapter 3
9 Gender Areas 27

Chapter 4
Area Characteristics 34

Chapter 5
Recognizing The Areas 63

Chapter 6
Basic Interferences 70

Pre-Chapter 7
Rooms & Meanings 77

Chapter 7
The Bedroom 79

Chapter 8
Bathroom & Toilet 111

Chapter 9
Kitchen & Dining Room 134

Chapter 10
The Living Room 156

Chapter 11
The Office 176

Chapter 12
Honorable Mentions 199

Chapter 13
The Elements &
Their Shapes 210

Chapter 14
Symmetry 222

Chapter 15
Summary & Index 228

Chapter 16
Readings By Aur 235

Chapter 17
Self-Quiz 247

Introduction

YOUR HOME REVEALS EVERYTHING ABOUT YOU details how unseen natural influences affect every person and their home. When understood, these forces provide great insight into our connection with the world around us. You will soon see how almost ever aspect of our lives is shaped by the structures in which we live and work.

We begin by sharing a little history of the unique style of Feng Shui discussed in this book and explaining its distinction from other schools of more commonly known Feng Shui. Next, we discuss the universal laws of interconnectivity, dualism, and karma, which we need to keep in mind while discussing this style of Feng Shui.

Then, you'll learn about nine distinct areas of influence found in any property, and their impact on any actions taken in those areas. After you're properly acquainted with each area and its characteristics, we connect them to the symbolic meaning of each room found in an average home.

Once combined, you'll gain a clear picture of those in the house, including their behavior, habits, and preferences.

In the later chapters, we add more dimension by revealing how the geometric shapes of land and houses have their own meaning and influence. Plus there's an opportunity to practice the theory shared in this book with short quizzes and real-life examples where Aur has shared her analysis of various floor plans sent to us by students.

We highly suggest walking around your home with this book and trying everything for yourself. Test the accuracy for yourself. Above all else, we want you to gain a firsthand experience of how your whole life is linked to your home, and see for yourself what this connection means for your relationships, finances, health and more.

By the time you finish this book, you'll know (among other things):

- ➢ How to predict anyone's personality & lifestyle within minutes, simply from their floorplan or home.
- ➢ How your bedroom influences your sex life, your sleeping patterns. And what you can do to improve your sleep.
- ➢ How a tiny change to the toilet can transform your financial life.
- ➢ How to pick the best restaurant every time, just from knowing where their kitchen is.
- ➢ How the shape of your home and land could be secretly holding you back from happy relationships.
- ➢ How to arrange your home office for optimum productivity.

CHAPTER 1
Connecting History

LET'S TAKE A MOMENT to talk about the jade elephant in the room. You've probably heard of Traditional Chinese Feng Shui. These days it's almost commonplace in any discussions of interior decoration and home design.

Maybe you're also even aware of Feng Shui tools like the Bagua wheel (prevalent in Chinese Feng Shui) which is used to maximize the "chi" flowing through your home. This is said to be important because harnessing this mystical power is said to harmonize you with the universe, improving your luck, and prosperity. Apparently.

Let's get straight to the point by making it clear that this book has nothing to do with that. At all. Seriously.

If you have studied Chinese Feng Shui in the past, or are a Chinese Feng Shui enthusiast, we'd kindly ask you to regard the knowledge within this book as an entirely separate area of study. Mixing the two will likely end in confusion.

Let's take a look at an example. It's common in modern or Traditional Chinese Feng Shui to believe that having water in a house is a good thing. Because it's said (amongst other things) to balance the five elements and increase prosperity.

Aur's Feng Shui sees this differently. Her style considers any water which isn't naturally present to be lacking qualities to maintain fresh life. In contrast to common belief, she teaches that placing a water feature within a house often makes people sick, emotional, and argumentative. Here's why.

Collected water allows the breeding of bacteria and germs. When exposed to heat or sunlight, the water gradually evaporates and carries these impurities into the air. When there's a body of water in the house, these bacteria and germs disperse throughout all the rooms. People living there will inevitably inhale these pollutants, which in turn affects their immune system. This predisposes them to more frequent illness. Additionally, the constant (however imperceptible) stress on their body will make them moody, which leads to arguments with others in the house.

As you can see, the understanding of these two vastly different forms of "Feng Shui" (literally meaning Water & Air) wisdom varies widely. However, the two do share a common history.

Long before the formation of China, a natural science emerged from the deserts of ancient Mesopotamia. This was when our early ancestors started attempting to channel and control the natural environment around their fixed settlements. Long before electricity and plumbing, they were forced to utilize their natural surroundings to provide themselves and their families with survival, comfort, good health, and a means of income.

It was during this time of old-fashioned ingenuity and early scientific exploration when they first discovered the existence of subtle repeating patterns and connections between the natural environment and their daily lives.

Over time through experimentation, our ancestors slowly learned how to harness the flow of nature itself. Armed with this knowledge, they created vast, thriving cities and shared their secrets to vitality, happiness, and wealth with others. They opened universities where they taught natural science and agricultural studies to people from all regions. In its day, Mesopotamia was the center of the civilized world.

As their studies and experiments continued, they came across even deeper dimensions and levels of nature, allowing them to do amazing things. It wasn't long before they were able to predict future events and know every detail about the life, or characteristic, of any human, plant, and animal on earth from the stars, natural elements, and universal patterns of life.

Over time, this blossoming natural science spread to neighboring regions including ancient Babylon, Egypt, and other surrounding areas. It inspired new sciences and art forms such as the creation of calendars, the design of magnificent architectural structures, and the creation of multiple alphabets and numerical systems. Our ancestors' understanding of nature's patterns and cycles was the spark igniting everything which followed.

Quick note: Our seven days of the week were initially named after planetary bodies due to their reoccurring patterns and influences on this planet. Sunday was the day of the Sun; Monday was the day of the Moon, and so on. However, the names and meanings of every day changed with each new dominant religion and culture, finally leaving us with mostly Scandinavian-influenced weekday names. In other books, we discuss how these planetary alignments for each day of the week allow us to know anyone's personality, with guaranteed accuracy. But that's for another time.

Unfortunately, the natural science fragmented categorically as it spread geographically, the direction and purity depending each time on the culture, religion and individual teachers sharing the knowledge. For example, those in the Mediterranean specialized in alphabetical and numerical systems. This branch created the origins of what is now known as Pythagorean numerology. Trade routes to the East helped shape the first concept of "Feng Shui" in early China.

Unfortunately, like most ancient wisdom, the perceived importance of our connection with nature was slowly replaced by the human species' inherent greed and its quest for power.

With the creation of empires, civilizations were destroyed, along with their wisdom. Similar to the loss of Native American and Aborigine cultures in recent history. Centuries long conflicts between nations diverted attention from classical education such as nature, and philosophy. People started favoring technological advancement, political development, and military strategy.

In the end, only a few branches of the fundamental holistic knowledge survived the sand of time. Chinese Feng Shui is an example of this. In China, Feng Shui became widely accepted to the point of becoming ingrained in their culture and remained at the forefront of daily life throughout the early development of the country.

But intellectual tragedy struck roughly 2,000 years ago when history repeated itself. Greed and power won yet again when the then rulers and governmental system in China ordered mass book burnings and the executions of most scholars, the extent of which resulted in the survival of only a handful of monks and royal advisors with authentic knowledge of the past. Feng Shui did and has remained a significant aspect of daily life for much of China, but it lost most of its authentic ancient lineage in this devastating event. It was sadly not the only time book burnings and executions happened in China either – the most recent was just last century.

Fragmentation and significant variations in interpretation of Feng Shui principals are the primary reasons why this book differs from what is known as Traditional Chinese Feng Shui. We don't follow the Chinese-lineage Feng Shui, which holds little connection to our ancestor's wisdom. Instead, we use a direct lineage from where it all started – the original Mesopotamian natural science.

Then and Now

Nature has stayed mostly the same in the last 10,000+ years. In contrast, our daily lives have changed drastically. It's simply unproductive to use the same advice as we would back then. We need to adapt to the time we in which we live.

There was a time when having water on a property would be good advice. Back when it flowed naturally in and out of a person's home or village. In those days, living near a water source meant that people could maintain good health and enjoy an abundance of food. It's for this reason that water is considered a good thing to have in our homes, according to Traditional Chinese Feng Shui. At one point in history, it was indeed useful advice.

But times have changed, and so have our homes. Structures aren't engineered the same way as they were; now we pump water into our homes. Maintaining a body of water on our property is no longer essential to the survival of our families. In fact, it's detrimental to our health, as mentioned previously.

Another significant change is in the design of our homes. Long before air-conditioning and glass windows, homes were designed to stay cool using the natural flow of wind. Houses were designed to allow sunlight into every corner of the house which killed bacteria, keeping people healthy. Every element of design had a reason and used nature to improve people's lives. This isn't true today. Most homes today are designed primarily for their look and often don't make the greatest use of airflow or sunlight. Instead, we use electricity to provide lighting and air conditioners or fans for airflow. We try our best to replace nature with technology. We gain comfort in the present moment but lose a lot in the process.

The following chapters look beyond design and engineering and reconnect our modern-day lives with the ancient knowledge of nature's unseen patterns and cycles. Everything to follow is to help you to understand and improve your life in some way, with quantifiable results.

CHAPTER 2
Fundamentals

Although completely natural, the perspectives we're about to discuss are vastly different than our normal thought processes used for modern day to day life. Before we get into it all, let's first discuss a few concepts, to settle our minds into the right framework. This will create a fertile mental ground to cultivate our understanding of nature's role in our lives from a fresh perspective.

The following "Fundamentals" section, consists of various underlying natural laws to keep in mind while reading this book, to provide you the mental groundwork for what is to come.

Interconnectivity

We are from every perspective connected to the world around us. This connection isn't esoteric, spiritual, or metaphorical. The undeniable truth is that we are psychologically, culturally, and biologically connected to everything around us.

A fundamental aspect of this connection is seen through the classical elements. Modern science has done an excellent job of categorizing the many reoccurring building blocks in life. Just look at the periodic table, and you'll see that there are over 100 elements, with more added just recently.

However, no matter how many elements we discover, they can always be categorized under the same four classical elements as outlined in Babylonian mythology, Greek philosophy, and ancient Buddhist scripture, namely:

Fire, Water. Earth, Air.

Everything around us, from the table at which we sit to the birds in the sky, or the phone in our pockets – are all made from the same four basic structural ingredients. Not only are they made of the same elements, but they interact with each other too. The moon influences the oceans. The sun affects the wind, which all interacts with the land and so on.

Our bodies are no different. They're combinations of the same ingredients as found in any other object. We're constantly in contact with other elements around us. Whether consciously or not, this communication between ourselves and the surrounding world influences our entire lives more ways than commonly thought.

Pause for a moment to consider that there is no more difference between the water found in your saliva or blood, than water found in the vast oceans or a rain droplet. Have you ever stopped to think that a minuscule amount of the same air you are breathing into your lungs right now was once Cleopatra's last breath? Or Gandhi's first? We all breathe the same air.

Even the teeny fire-like electrical pulses, running through your body, facilitating thought and consciousness, providing you the ability to feel and experience, can be found in any plant or animal on this planet. It's the same fire.

We can look at this connective commonality from any perspective, in any dimension. Elemental characteristics are even the intangible realm of emotions. We all know the intense heat of anger or the warmth of passion. Our bodies literally heat up in these moments. This isn't coincidental. The same four elements are what create life.

Colors have their elements too. Most interior decorators will say that red is a warm and passionate color creating motion, whereas blue is a subdued color. We all know what elements come to mind when hearing these characteristics too. Everyone knows intuitively that red is fire and blue, water.

The further we look into our world's simple elemental makeup, the more we begin to understand how even the smallest things in our lives have such power to transform us. We discover how everything, even colors, connect to our health, emotions, love life, family, career, personal wealth, and most every other area of our lives.

Surrounding Influences

Following along the same theme, we can start to see that nothing happens independently. Everything is affected by everything else.

Imagine a grapevine. We can make a clear distinction between the vine itself, the soil under it, the air around it, other neighboring plants and so on. From this observation, we would be right to say that the vine is an individual organism with separate natural processes and unique characteristics.

Why is it then that each wine tastes so different? Even when from the same grape variety or the same farm. They should be the same, but they aren't. Any farmer will tell you that the characteristics of any plant's shape, growth, color, and flavor, all depend on its surroundings. Even the time it is planted changes everything. Viticulturalists have used this knowledge for thousands of years in the quest to create unique superior wine varieties.

The truth is, everything in the vines vicinity affects the character of the grape. If a farmer uses coffee grinds as fertilizer, the coffee will decompose, but the soil will maintain certain enzymes and minerals that affect the grape's flavor, growth, and color. Likewise, the wind carries whatever it passes. This is why disease amongst plants most commonly spreads downwind. A warm wind will affect the grapes one way, cold, another. Other trees around the vine effect the vine too. They'll feed on the soil and deposit their own chemicals and minerals back into the earth, in turn, influencing the grape vine.

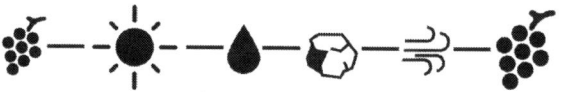

The once considered lone grape vine no longer seems separate. In fact, the line between characteristics unique to the plant and those resulting from surrounding influences starts to blur.

Humans are not unlike the metaphorical grapevine. From our point of view, we seem to be single, self-sustaining organisms. But when observed objectively, you can start to see how profoundly influenced we are by our environment. Everything around us impacts our lives in one way or another. Although we typically don't think about it or know how to use it to our advantage.

The problem is that, at a societal level, we maintain the illusion that we are different from nature, superior in some way. In reality, we are each just the four natural elements, bundled together temporarily in this form we like to call "me." We're biologically no different from anything else in this world.

Two Dimensions of Influence

There are two distinct levels of interaction between ourselves and our surroundings. One is the "tangible" world that we can quantify through our physical senses. We can see, touch, taste, smell, hear and feel it at a macro level. An example of a substantial influence is the moon's influence on our planet's water. We are all aware that the moon's gravitational pull forces all water on earth, including the water in our bodies, to move in certain ways. However, science still falls short when sharing how something like this pertains to our daily lives.

The other level is that of intangible influences, which is a little harder to define. For thousands of years, various ancient religious and mystic texts have claimed that existence is shaped by the mind itself, and is in itself not real. However, we are only now discovering the same thing through science, using modern systems such as quantum physics. Science is an excellent tool. However, it still has limitations due to its focus on the physical, sensory realms of existence.

Intangible influences are everything we cannot connect to our physical senses. Such as how the colors we wear, changes our lives, or how the positioning of the stars have a direct impact on our personalities and choices in life. Ethereal effects are not invisible; they are simply more subtle and indirectly perceivable than what we consider substantial influences. The color t-shirt you wear today may seem insignificant or minor. But remember, it is the splitting of the tiniest atom which creates both nuclear power for millions, or the destruction of entire cities. Just because something may seem insignificant, doesn't mean its power is.

Example: Tangible Influences

Most take airflow for granted in a world with fans and air-conditioning, but it's often a large aspect of a skilled architect's decision-making process.

For example, if an area doesn't have natural airflow, there will be a rise in temperature and a lack of fresh oxygen, causing people to become irritable and to feel uncomfortable there. If the area is your home, poor airflow can result in tensions between people in the family. The house will be experienced as an uncomfortable environment, which in a worst-case scenario could eventually lead to separation.

A business or office without adequate airflow will result in low staff productivity, and ultimately affect the organization's success. If you don't have access to fresh and oxygen-rich air, your brain won't function properly. Therefore, people in a building lacking airflow will not be able to perform at full mental capacity.

Example: Intangible Influences

As we know, everything is made from the same elements. These elements move in the same flow and patterns. The forces and cycles that apply to the cosmos, our solar system, and our planet, also apply to ourselves. But on a more subtle scale.

On a planetary level, the various forces of nature create seasons with their particular characteristics. These distinct yearly cycles are shaped on a macro level. But, because everything is connected and with common origins, it is also true that we go through seasons in our lives. Each year of our lives is different. Some years, everything will seem to flow, whereas others, everything seems to go in the opposite direction than what we thought. It's not just the years of our lives which move in predictable patterns. Ever day is part of the cycle.

One day we will wake up feeling great, and want to be social, other days we feel that we want to be alone. We usually call these "moods." But modern society doesn't explain what they are. In essence, moods are straightforward signs of the four element's natural cycles within our bodies.

This is why, when understood, we can know how our lives will be at any point in time. Some call it psychic ability or fortunetelling. However, it's more akin to being able to predict the weather for any given December within the last 100 years. In the Northern Hemisphere it will be cold, Southern will be hot. You don't need a six sense to know that. It's science.

When you understand your own life seasons, you become aware of and prepared for both the good times and the bad.

Duality and Beyond

Nothing in life is only good. Nor can it only be bad. Everything has two sides. If one exists, the other must too. If there is happiness, sadness must exist too. If there is light, there's dark. It's the dichotomic universe we live in.

Quick Note: As we also know, nothing is separate. Opposites, like night and day, are also connected. This is why the Ying and Yang symbol has the small circle in each half. It reminds us that even in the darkest night, there is light, that in poison there is medicine, and in death there is life. Every is like this – a beautiful play of symbiosis, enhancing, and complementing each other.

According to ancient Mesopotamian texts, the creation of the yin and yang forces are what created the universe in the first place. They believed that in the beginning, there was only the formless, infinite, from where the two opposing forces of masculinity and femininity suddenly appeared, creating everything after that. Sounds similar to the Big Bang theory, right?

The two forces exist on all levels of existence, both tangible and intangible. Our own physical bodies and behavioral representations are a reflection of that universal law and just one example. Actually, this dichotomy is at the core of why our homes reveal everything about us. But first, let's look at what masculinity and feminity are, in the easiest form we can understand. Gender.

Gender Duality

There is much research and debate in today's society as to what the core gender roles and stereotypes are. It is, in fact, a touchy subject, full of politically correct censorship due to personal opinions and values. In the end, each and every individual is different, with significant influences from upbringing, culture, career, personality and so on. If we look into nature for a general, rule of thumb depiction of the gender roles, we are able to collect generalizations about each of the sexes. Some may feel that these characteristics don't specifically apply to their personalities. Remember, they're merely a general guide to the gender traits. We'll use these general characteristics later.

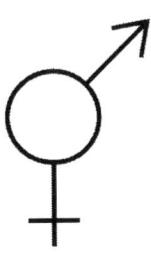

Masculinity

Consider for a moment, what masculinity is. This would be hard to do if we only examined masculinity in humans. No person is 100% masculine. Every male will have both feminine and masculine aspects of their personality. It's better to look beyond the human species to the signs of pure masculinity in the natural world.

Biological

From a purely microbiological aspect, we can see that high levels of the hormone called testosterone correlates with many male behavioral characteristics, and is considered the determining male hormone in many species. It's found in significantly higher concentrations within the males of any animal.

What does testosterone do? Elevated levels of testosterone can increase aggressive or assertive behavior, improve visual-spatial ability and judgment, lead to poorer concentration and heightened anxiety, increased sexual appetite (but not increased the desire for touching), and an increased sense of separateness. These are simply traits characteristic of testosterone, but we can draw a picture of pure masculine characteristics from this.

Behavioural

Let's look at general male behavior. By observing most male animals, we know that men tend to be highly protective and possessive. Ownership seems an important aspect of security and survival for the male gender. We see many species where males demonstrate violent and territorial behavior. Many will kill to keep what's theirs, or to take what they want. This shows high importance regarding ownership. Many species also tend to control their surroundings through maintaining skillful dominance. In general, males want authority and seek the maximum level of power in their realm. We see that many males will often fight to gain social rank in their groups. The males in most species are commonly selfish, individualistic and self-centered. You more often see the male species tending to live alone or fending for itself. These are all traits commonly seen in almost any species.

Universal

What about universal, non-gender based, masculine characteristics? If we imagine the simple definitions of any male object, animate or not, we gain further insight into what masculinity is. When thinking of universal masculinity qualities, what words would you use? Many think of words like strong, sizable, stable, focused, single-tasked, logical, specialist, or unchanging. Perhaps you may have others comes to mind. That's great, the clearer your picture of the masculine and feminine is, the better your understanding will be of what's next.

One thing to keep in mind is that all species with male traits won't express them in the same way. The underlying masculine motivations for actions and thoughts will first pass through various filters which determine the final action or thought. Filters include species, culture (environment), age, and gender (all females have masculine qualities too).

Example: All males may be protective of their property, but a male dog may physically attack another male who comes into his territory, whereas a human male may only use verbal communication if feeling threatened, or if they're very young, they may simply cry.

Femininity

What is femininity? Again if we only look at people's outer personalities, it can get confusing. There is both masculinity and femininity in any female. So let's again break it down into purer gender forms.

BIOLOGICAL

If we return to the microbiological position, estrogen is the associated predominant "feminine" hormone. No matter which species we look at, a female of that species will always have more estrogen than testosterone. Whereas for males, it's vice versa. So, what characteristics are estrogen related to? In women, higher levels of estrogen increase their physical beauty and attractiveness, such as the texture and clarity of their skin, as well as their body odor. It also enhances concentration, heightens sensory acuity, improves memory and cognition, and creates a stable state of well-being.

BEHAVIOURAL

From a behavioral aspect, we can find signature characteristics to most, if not all female species. A widely universal feminine trait is a tendency towards being highly protective of offspring and those they love. For example, a female wolf protects her partner's throat when another male threatens him. Almost every mother has an innate maternal bond with their babies. The father doesn't usually share this same bond.

Another feminine behavioral characteristic is the particular sense of connection and community with peers they seem to have. Females of nearly all species are more socially inclusive than their male counterparts. Where males may be more risk-taking and easily bored, women tend to be more comfortable in routine activities and more skilled at detail-oriented activities.

Universal

As for universal feminine characteristics, words such as softness, nurturing, beauty, change, small, cycles, nature, and intuitive may come to mind. Or perhaps you can think of other characteristics for universal femininity, which is great too. Again, the clearer picture, the better.

Beyond Dichotomy

The moment night and day become one, breathtaking dawns and romantic dusks are created. These moments are in themselves different from either day or night, while simultaneously being both. In the world of duality, there is always a third where the two meet. In humans (and other species) this blend of masculine and feminine are most easily seen in gay, lesbian, bisexual, transgender, or hermaphrodite individuals. They have qualities particular to both genders, but also something unique that neither side has on their own. We call this blend of the two, the third sex. Understanding this third aspect of nature is integral to learning how to correctly interpret Feng Shui.

All humans, no matter their sexual orientation, could be considered third sex. No person is purely masculine or purely feminine either. Every person, regardless of gender, has both masculine and feminine qualities. People may have more of one than the other, but both are always influencing our thoughts and actions. Sometimes we'll follow our more masculine side, other times we'll think and act more aligned with femininity. This is why we can see the third-sex as a representation for human beings.

For most people, whether we act more masculine or feminine depends mostly on our moods. Our temporary emotions are one of the largest determinants for what we choose at any given moment. As you will see, this is a core characteristic of the third sex personality. With both masculine and feminine blended into something unique of itself, a prime feature of the third-sex is the ability to think and see the world differently than others. That's why creativity is a fundamental component of the third-sex profile.

One other important aspect of the 3-rd sex character to keep in mind their tendency towards privacy. On average, the third gender doesn't like to share personal details about who they are, especially to their family. Almost every human has some sense of boundaries of aspects of themselves that they do not want to share with others. They may feel it might make them look bad or that it may not be accepted by the ones they love, but most humans have this boundary of privacy between who they truly are and the outside world. Now, let's look at the next fundamental concept, karma.

Karma

Everything in your life - right now - is a direct result of your actions, thoughts, and feelings in the past. Karma is the notion of the eternal continuation of action and reaction. It's the underlying current of our lives.

What makes any person different from the other is the karma they create for themselves through their actions, thoughts, and feelings. In essence, the culmination of our choices in the past have created our present life, and what we chose to do in the present moment becomes our future. This is what we call karma. Everyone is precisely where their karma has led them to be.

People who believe in reincarnation may see karma as a connection throughout many lives and believe that someone who suffers in this life must have done something wrong in a past life. But, it isn't necessary to believe in reincarnation to see how karma works. Karma is plainly visible in this life.

For example, we can say that it is Bill Gate's karma to be as financially wealthy as he is. But for others like you and I, our karma doesn't permit that. Why? Because we do not have the same thoughts, actions, and feelings that he has. It is who he is and what he has thought, and done in his earlier years, which has brought him to where he is today. Similarly, we have placed ourselves where we are today, too.

In contrast, karma is often thought of in the sense that, if you do something evil, a similar wrong will later happen to you. This is true too. For example, if someone lies often, we could say this is creating bad karma. Why? People will be less likely to believe that individual in the future, which creates suffering. They become more isolated from others and lose authentic relationships. This is why we call it bad karma, because the result they end up with, is unpleasant. If instead, the person chose to speak honestly at all times, they would gain a reputation for honesty and trustworthiness, resulting in authentic relationships and trust from those around them. That would be good karma.

In a different scenario, imagine a person who spends much of their time intoxicating themselves with alcohol or drugs. Over time, their mental and physical functioning will deteriorate, causing loss of health and possibly an early death. This is, of course, a very specific and extreme case. But it's another example of how karma can be seen in everything we do. Like it or not, karma is created with every action, thought or feeling we create, and it influences our entire life.

Karma is closely connected to the concept of a personality. If you study psychology, you learn that a personality is simply a relatively persistent pattern of thoughts, actions, feelings, and choices. We can change it. But usually, we subconsciously repeat the same cycles. Our actions create reactions which again produce new actions and so on.

This is why we continually create the same situations in our lives, and why the symbol for karma is a never-ending loop. Consciously and subconsciously, we habitually place ourselves in the same circumstances and environments which harvest the same results, over and over again. That's what leads us to pick similar romantic partners over and over, find similar jobs, or eat the same foods over and over. This is what we call "following our karma."

What people don't know, is that they're unwittingly drawn to pick similar places to live over and over again which also support the continuation of the cycles they live in. This is why, once you're able to see how your home is influencing your life, you're able to use it to break out of negative cycles and experience real change in your life.

Now that we've covered the fundamentals, it's time to delve into the details of how the structures we live and work in influence our lives.

CHAPTER 3
9 Gender Areas

Your home is a representation of your life. Your home reveals your personality, habits, and lifestyles. Once understood, you can see everything about a person, simply from their home. But, maybe not in the way you'd expect.

Each room in a house represents an area of the inhabitant's life. For example, a bedroom reveals their sleep routines, personality, and sexual habits. Whereas the living room expresses their social life and how they interact with visitors in the house. How we interpret each room depends on its location within the house. This is because every building in the world has distinct unseen areas of influence which affect our any action, thought and feelings differently, depending on where we are within that structure.

Similarly to our own brains and bodies, ever structure in the world has a masculine and feminine side. Across the world, the right aspect of a property will be affected by masculine qualities. Any activities in that area, or uses for those areas, will be somehow impacted by masculine traits. Whereas the left-hand side of any space is influenced by feminine characteristics. Directly down the middle, wedged between the masculine and feminine areas, is the third sex area.

An area's ultimate effect depends on many factors. In particular, we have to look at the utility of the area which we are analyzing, and what this space symbolizes in a person's life. Then, we look at the individual who will be using that space. The influence a property has over them will differ depending on their career, age, sex, culture, and belief system. This is because these factors play a significant role in shaping an individual's personality. Let's start by looking further into the areas and their meaning.

The 9 Gender Areas

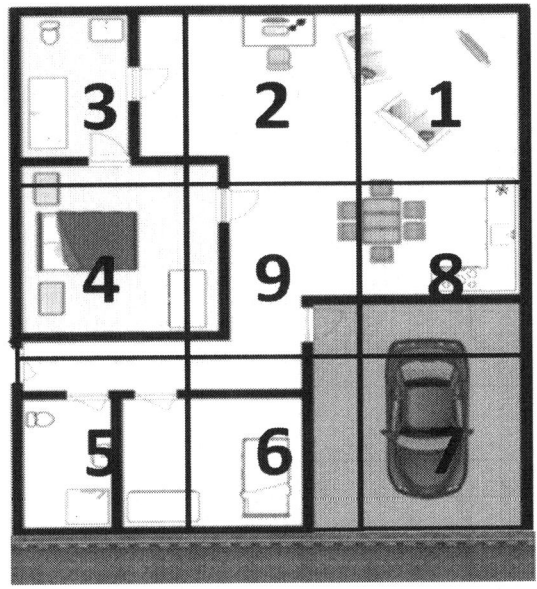

The 9 distinct areas of influence found within any structure can be divided up similar to a TIC-TAC-TOE board, like the picture above. The positions of these 9 zones are the same everywhere in the world, no matter the country, culture or belief structure. This system of 9 gender areas can be applied to homes or businesses, virtually every property on earth.

The Masculine Areas (1, 8, 7)

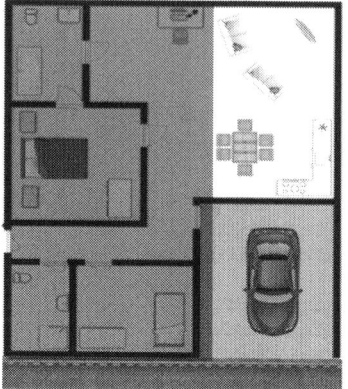

The right area of every property is influenced by natural male characteristics. As you can see, there are three distinct zones within the male area. The back of a property, where the number 1 is, is the area associated with an adult male. Any activity or use for that area will be affected by characteristics as seen in a universal adult male.

These influences will be very different from the 8 area. Although it's also in the masculine area, the 8 area has its own unique characteristic traits. This space represents the teenage boy character. Peoples' actions in this area will somehow be associated with an adolescent male's personality and psychological characteristics. As you may guess, the 7 area at the front of the property represents the boy, whose character is very different from both an adult male and a teenage male. Although each one is unique, all the masculine areas will have similarities, just like their personas. Activities throughout the male areas are more likely driven by sensual motivations, more big picture and imaginative than their female counterparts, and focused on new and challenging things, rather than routine.

The Feminine Areas (3, 4, 5)

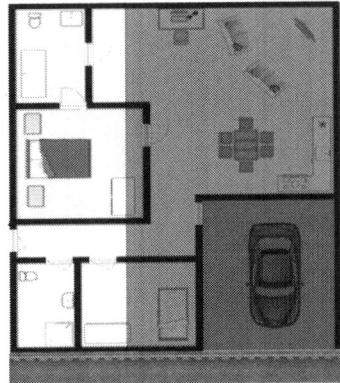

Similarly, the left 'feminine' side consists of the adult woman personality in the back left 3 area, the teenage girl in area 4, and the girl in the 5 area at the front. Interactions with objects and rooms in those areas will be influenced by feminine forces. But, as you can imagine, the influences of an adult woman's characteristics would differ substantially from those of a young girl.

In contrast to the masculine zones, activities in the feminine areas will be more emotionally driven and focused on stability and familiarity, rather than 'new' things. They'll be more concerned with how something looks, than actions taken in the male areas. Actions there are likely done with more attention to detail, in a more organized fashion than their male counterparts.

The 3rd-Sex Areas (2, 6)

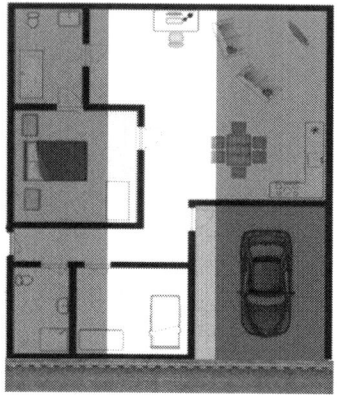

3	2	1
4	9	8
5	6	7

The three third-sex areas are in-between the masculine and feminine areas. Remember, this area doesn't only represent a mixture of the masculine AND feminine qualities, it has its own uniqueness, distinct from both. Just as the masculine and feminine areas, the adult characteristics will be at the back of the property, in the 2 area. Whereas the 6 area at the front of a house represents a 3rd-sex child, who is different from either boys or girls. The 9 area in the middle of a building special. We'll get to that soon.

The key features associated with actions in the 2 and 6 areas will be that people think differently, keep a level of privacy, are often misunderstood by others, and are guided by mood.

The Family Area (9)

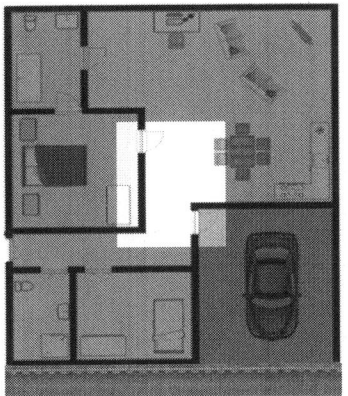

3	2	1
4	9	8
5	6	7

The center 9 position represents both the teenage, third-sex, but more importantly, the family area. This is where all the influences from the surrounding areas join together to form a whole new set of characteristics. The best symbolic representation of this area is that of a large family. Anything in this area cannot only involve one person. That's not what we would call a family. By definition, this area has to be used by multiple people. This is a space which continuously attracts problems, but which also has the most power. It depends on how you use it.

Let's continue by first discussing each areas' personality in more detail and giving you some keywords to keep in mind when looking at each of the 9 areas. Then we will be able to connect each area to different rooms in a house and explain - in detail - how they directly influence specific areas of our lives. The next section would be a good place to keep a bookmark or note, so you are able to quickly revisit it when needed.

CHAPTER 4
Area Characteristics

Now that you know the different areas of influence in a property or structure, let's delve into each area one by one, and look at the particular ways in which they impact our behavior, habits, and lifestyles. For each area, we'll discuss its personality, giving you an overview of the character, and provide examples along the way to illustrate how to interpret that areas impact on our day-to-day life. Each section also has a list of general characteristics to keep in mind when looking at each area. This will help when analyzing a property. Try to find each of the 9 areas in your own home to get used to recognizing where they are in a building.

#1. The Man Area

3	2	1
4	9	8
5	6	7

The number 1 area symbolizes an adult male. Every activity in this area will be influenced by traits associated with the universally recognized "typical adult male." Every man is very different on the surface but will share deeper commonalities. These common personality traits found in men around the world are what form the essential characteristics for this area.

To be clear, a woman or child performing some kind of activity in this space won't start to act like a man. Every one of us has personality traits associated with a stereotypical male, no matter our age or gender. These will be emphasized when in the number 1 area of a property. This is why it's crucial to take the actual person into account for whom we are analyzing the areas of influence. A young girl's behavior in this space would be very different from an adult man. However, they will have similar masculine motivators driving their behavior.

Generic qualities of an adult male found in everyone, which will be emphasized in this area, are things such as competitiveness, territoriality, and possessiveness.

There'll be a heightened desire to be in charge and important when in this area. A good thing about this area is that it can enhance a person's ability to make decisions quickly, and logically rather than being emotionally driven. But, people are more likely to be messy, bored quickly, to dislike routine, and only focus on one thing at a time, unless they command others to do something for them (imagine a head chef in a kitchen).

When considering what other specific influences the man area may have on one's behavior, it's useful to place the character of a typical male in different situations, depending on the use of the area. For example, when looking at a living room in this area, try to imagine when a man is with his friends, does he enjoy being with a small group of friends or a large group of friends? Generally, men will enjoy large group activities whereas women will prefer being with just a few close friends.

Or what if the area is used for scheduling activities for the day. Do men on average like to plan every detail, or are they more spontaneous? Usually, men prefer taking action over planning. But remember, it also depends on the person using the space. If a woman is in this area, she is likely to still continue planning, but it won't be in detail.

Note: Getting used to stereotypical characters takes some practice. To gain a clearer view of the sexes, it's always handy to put them in many different situations to understand their behavioral habits. For example, try thinking about how males act in social settings, or when faced with an argument, sleeping, working, cooking and so forth.

#1. General Characteristics:

- Heated Temper
- Spontaneous
- Likes to be "cool."
- Competitive
- Social but private
- Flashy / Grandiose
- Lazy in Personal Life
- Deep sleeper (but hard to get to sleep)
- Commanding
- Hates being told what to do.
- Territorial/ Possessive
- Dislikes doing the same thing over and over again
- Large quantities
- Single-minded/Focused
- Wants everything fast
- Big picture
- Sensual/Tactile
- Takes Charge
- Loves new things
- Loves new technology
- Protective
- Likes socializing
- Unorganised
- Doesn't think in detail
- Procrastinator
- Straight to the point

- Logical
- Assertive
- Open-minded
- High Ego
- Easily bothered by others
- Highly Work-Oriented
- Ambitious

#2. 3rd-Sex Adult Area

3	2	1
4	9	8
5	6	7

The adult 3rd-sex persona is identified by the number 2 area. Before discussing the associated characteristics of this area, it's important to understand that every characteristic as a purely natural phenomenon, separate from personal opinion.

It can be challenging at first for some people learning the areas of influence, due to the social stigma around the idea of stereotyping. Especially when in the case of sexual orientation, when we use gay and lesbian stereotypes to better understand the third sex area.

Keep in mind that when looking at the good or bad within a person's house that we're not judging anyone by personal opinion. We simply use the general characteristics or stereotypes to acknowledge the character traits and use them to quantify natural influences around us. Regardless whether people claim that generalization is a good or a bad thing, the fact is that these archetypical forces exist in nature and are useful tools in the learning experience.

Every human being has both male and female traits so we could use a general adult human being as our stereotypical character. However, it's difficult for most people to generalize the third-sex as people. It's too broad for most to imagine. To compensate, we use the symbolic character concept of the average gay man, lesbian woman or transgender individual, which provides a clearer picture. They're a natural blend of masculine and feminine forces, which combine together to create something completely unique in itself. A perfect example of the third-sex.

For example, in general, gay men will be more in touch with their emotions, they will show higher levels of creativity and see things very differently than most straight men. At the same time, they covet their privacy, preferring not to share certain details of their lives with others, especially their family.

A lesbian woman will similarly have personality traits from both feminine and masculine sides. They can be exceptionally emotional with big hearts. But, usually don't want to show their true feelings to others, similar to how a man feels. They like to keep their lives private too. They tend to be deep thinkers and think differently than others. On average, most 3rd-sex adults prefer to spend most of their time with like-minded people, who see things as they do.

For the third-sex character, emotions are center stage. Accordingly, any activity performed in this area of a property will highly depend on the mood or feelings of the person conducting the activity. Because their emotions are fluid, it's difficult for them to make a decision if their emotions are involved. For example, they cannot be neutral when making decisions involving the people they love (or hate). Third-sex characters are people who love can love something to death but hate to death too.

A good thing about the third-sex character is that, when they leave their emotions our of it, they are able to think in unique, creative, and different ways. They have access to both feminine and masculine perspectives.

#2. General Characteristics:

- Doesn't like change
- Doesn't accept being wrong
- Wants attention
- Wants acceptance/ admiration
- High importance on appearances/aesthetic
- Cannot control their emotions
- Only close to those they trust
- Highly private personal life
- Always changing in mood and emotions

- Does everything based on how they feel at the moment
- Biased based on their own feelings
- Like to be in the spotlight
- Nagging, critiquing,
- Highly opinionated.
- Don't talk unless they have shared interests
- Emotional
- Thinks differently
- Imaginative & Creative
- Annoyed easily
- Individualistic

#2 Area Quick Example

Let's say a dining room were to be in this zone, and that a family of four lived in this house. If so, we would be able to say they would all sit together, but wouldn't talk much over dinner. If they did talk, it would likely be small talk and nothing about their personal issues or lives unless they had some kind of mutual interest, such as the son and father liking action-hero movies.

#3. The Woman Area

3	2	1
4	9	8
5	6	7

The 3 area at the back left of a property or structure is governed by adult female characteristics. When looking at this area in a house, all actions, thoughts, and feelings will be somehow influenced by traits associated with an adult female.

If we look at the mature female of any species to find generalizations, we can see that women are (on average) naturally detail-oriented, relationship-focused, and like to things to be in predictable patterns. They are more comfortable with routines than their male counterparts. They're are also more emotional, and fiercely protective of those they love (especially their children).

Women are usually continuously active, always alert to multiple things happening around them and mentally active. However they are also more self-critical, and in moments of high emotional tension often act and speak in ways opposite to how they feel. Although most women will see themselves as simple, good listeners and not picky, it usually isn't so.

They are dominant like their male counterparts but in different ways. An adult woman knows how to use their words and social influence to control others, rather than men who are more likely to use straight forward dominance or authority.

From a subjective view, we know that most females are protective of their familial and social environment rather than territorial over physical possession like males. Women are more nurturing than their male counterparts, providing safety and structure for their offspring. In humans, we can categorize this into characteristics such as being motherly, risk-averse and organized in basic routines.

Keep in mind that the effect this area will have on people differs depending on the inhabitant. A man sleeping in this area will often be softer and more emotional in personality than the average male. But, they'll also be more nagging and focused on detail than the average male. On the other hand, the average woman sleeping in this area is likely to have heightened feminine traits such as being highly detail-oriented, risk-averse, with little spontaneity and most comfortable when following a set routine.

#3 Area Quick Example

If a bathroom is in the woman's area of influence, you can be certain they would keep it clean, tidy and organized. They'll do a lot of things while in there. For example, tidy up, re-apply makeup, and do their hair.

#3. General Characteristics:

- Loves Romance and intimacy
- Self-expressive
- Highly detail-oriented
- Picky
- Thinks (& changes) fast
- Wants everything fast. --Impatient.
- Emotionally driven
- Neat & Clean
- Protective
- Responsible
- Gossipy
- Nagging
- Highly Loyal
- Gets into other's business.
- Often feels lonely or neglected.
- Loves company.
- Loves everything to be structured and organized
- Likes routine
- Deep sleeper but up early.
- Regular bedtimes
- Plans ahead
- Multi-tasking
- Micro-managing
- Self-critical
- Sensitive to criticism
- Always thinking of others

- Always taking care of others
- Maintains an excellent Image
- Appearance is everything
- Cannot explain their emotions

#4. Teenage Girl Area

3	2	1
4	9	8
5	6	7

Teen years are transformative. So many things change for people as they move through this period in their lives. It's the time when they can become anything they want in life. But, at the same time, many teenagers feel social and emotional pressure to act in certain ways. They are faced with the idea of becoming an adult while worrying about who they are, where they fit in, and what others think of them.

Teenage girls spend a lot of time focusing on what they look like to others. They want to look good in the eyes of their peers. Teenage girls feel pressured by the need for social approval from those around them. So they try to act mature, or what they believe mature to be. But, they still have mood swings like any teenager, which makes them prone to quickly becoming emotional or angry. Teenage girls also tend to keep their personal and family lives separate from their social lives.

Most teenage girls take responsibility more seriously than their male counterparts. When we look at the academic performance of teenagers, we see that on average, girls are more likely to excel at academics. It's not necessarily that girls are smarter than the boys (although they may think so). Teenage girls are more focused on what they believe is their individual responsibility and what will reap benefits for themselves, rather than their male peers. On average, they enjoy reading or anything to do with books more than boys do too. Although they may not enjoy it, teenage girls are more willing to do routine work, follow the rules, and fulfill their individual duties. They're are able to do almost anything with the right guidance.

#4. Quick Example:

It's a good thing to have a home office in the teenage girl area if you want to keep up with paperwork. A workspace in this space means that whoever is there will be good at paperwork and organizing things. They'll be diligent and very organized. However, if someone needs to create new things, or if they are in sales and have to speak to a lot of people every day, a desk in this area would not be a good thing for them.

#4. General Characteristics:

- Follows peers
- Good at routine (dislikes it)
- Good with paperwork
- Emotional but tries not to show it.
- Gullible
- Wants attention
- Argumentative
- Slow to trust others.
- Works hard (but dislikes it)
- Responsible
- Short-tempered
- Vain
- Won't make significant decisions by themselves.
- Likes to buy cute things
- Likes things that make them feel attractive.
- Needs structure & rules.
- Requires organization.
- Private with personal life
- Never sees big picture
- Clean but untidy/messy
- Not good with change.
- Can do almost anything but won't be the best at it.
- Doesn't understand their own emotions.

#5. Young Girl Area

3	2	1
4	9	8
5	6	7

The area at the front left of a property is associated with the young girl personality. As we all know, from watching movies and young girls in our families or social circles, every young girl has her own world, full of colorful characters who all follow her lead. Her world is important to her, and she wants you to recognize its importance too.

Imagine the cliché of having an imaginary tea party for hours at which you're expected as a guest. While sipping tea with Teddy and Dolly, the young girl creates vivid scenarios and step-by-step instructions on what everyone must do. Don't dare disagree unless you'd like to experience her wrath.

They are little dreamers and rulers in their dreams. Little girls know what they want and don't mind telling others what needs to be done. When in a comfortable and familiar environment, a young girl is a force to be reckoned with and will fight bravely for what she believes to be right. She's incredibly stubborn. It's tough for anyone to change her mind. But, in an unfamiliar setting, she'll be the opposite.

Withdrawn, quiet and sometimes distressed. Overall, young girls don't like new places or new people.

As with any child, young girls don't like to sit still. In the past, this could be interpreted to mean that whoever is using this space wouldn't stay in one place for long. But, now with the advent of the internet and smart devices, if someone does stay in a child position for long, you know they'll be mentally elsewhere. Either with the internet of their phone. Whatever they're doing though will usually change quickly according to how they feel, though. Because, to a young girl, her feelings how she decides everything she does.

Any action performed in this area is influenced by certain girl-like characteristics. Although again it depends on the person, and the use of the space itself.

#5. Quick Example:

If a bathroom is in the #5 young girl area, we can assume that the room will be clean, but untidy. Whoever uses this bathroom wouldn't spend much time in there. They'll be in and out.

#5. General Characteristics:

- Highly Creative
- Daydreamer
- Bossy
- Desires attention
- Seeks emotional affirmation
- Does everything by emotions
- Clumsy
- Often breaks things.
- Becomes emotionally fixated
- Always thinks about future
- Good with routine tasks
- Unorganized but thinks they are organized.
- Expects recognition
- Good with things they are familiar with.
- Not good with handling change
- To emotionally feel good is most important
- Averse to risk-taking.
- Loves safety and similarity.
- Think they are detail-oriented, but aren't.
- Don't like to take responsibility.
- Always active, always moving around.
- Lazy, and will try to get others to do things for them.
- Often thinks things are valuable when others don't.
- Wants to be a perfectionist but always makes mistakes.

#6. Young 3rd Sex Area

3	2	1
4	9	8
5	6	7

At the front and center area of a property, you will find the #6 young 3rd-sex area. So any action performed here is influenced by similar characteristics as seen in a young gay, lesbian or transgender child.

Consider for a second what the characteristics may be for a third-sex child. Growing up in a world where you feel different and out of place isn't easy. Especially at such a young age. The people around you don't seem to understand you, or even like the same things you do. At the same time, you don't know or understand yourself quite yet either, and can't figure out why you are different from others. Most children learn social skills by interacting with their peers, but for the third-sex child, even peers their age, who they look for to get an idea of how to fit in, all like different things than they do. Life for a young 3rd-sex individual is not comfortable. It can be a confusing and lonely time. They know they are different, but don't know yet how to express themselves coherently.

Third-sex children are usually highly intelligent, but often feel under-appreciated nor taken seriously for their intelligence, simply because the way they think is just so different from others. They're usually private but loyal those who love them for who they are.

General characteristics of anyone's behavior in this area of a house or business include being very private, quick to help others close to them and do everything for those they love. People here are often the ones doing all the work. The sad thing is that they're usually overlooked by others, and their work isn't often appreciated. For this reason, they frequently end up with tasks that no one else wants to do.

#6. General Characteristics:

- When they talk, others don't understand them.
- Quiet/Unsocial
- Private/Withdrawn
- Slow to trust others
- Never uses things around them.
- Never says "no" to others.
- Can't make decisions
- Short-Tempered
- Feels misunderstood/ unappreciated
- Usually by themselves
- In their own world
- Often anxious or stressed.
- People notice them but don't see the value of them.
- Does a good job, especially when familiar with it.
- Intelligent

- Wants to show off
- Lacking in confidence
- Exaggerates

#6. Quick Example:

If you see a house with the kitchen in the 3rd-sex child area, you can know for certain that it won't be used at all except for heating up a meal or making tea. People living here like to eat elsewhere.

#7. Young Boy Area

3	2	1
4	9	8
5	6	7

The area at the front right of a house is the young boy's zone. All behavior here will be influenced by a young boy's characteristics. Imagine a typical boy. Above all else, a young boy loves to play and have fun. He loves being boisterous, playful, and trying new things. But, he also gets bored quickly and continuously looks for something new.

For a young boy, doing things that aren't fun or spontaneous are just too boring to even do in the first place. They hate routine and anything to do with numbers, books or paperwork. It's not in their character. They won't be good at anything that requires patience or things that move slowly. Boys enjoy fast and exciting things. The good thing is that they're creative at coming up with new ways to enjoy themselves and do whatever is fun at the moment.

But, if you look away for even a moment, he will get up to some kind of mischief. As they say, silence is golden, until you have a young boy. Then silence becomes suspicious. You never know what he could get up to.

Young boys like to make themselves look good in front of their peers. They enjoy showing off how talented and independent they are. They're excellent at creating elaborate scenarios to show off their greatness.

But no matter how hard they try to look independent, the truth is that they're dependent and clingy to their custodians, family, or caregivers, and are secretly scared of taking risks.

Just like a young girl, you'll rarely see a boy sitting still. In the past, being in this area meant that a person wouldn't be able to stay in one place for long, just like an energetic boy. But as you know, we can now move our minds without moving our bodies with the Internet and all the devices available. Another new change is that boys now trust the internet more than the people around them!

A bad thing about this area is that young boys are usually messy and never clean up after themselves. It's common for things in this area to be untidy. The young boy character also represents being terrible with money management. If your toilet is in the wrong position in this area, there's a 90% chance you're in debt. But we'll talk more about that later.

#7. Quick Example:

A quick cautious note. If a couple sleeps in this area, there's a significant chance the man is sleeping with someone else too. It doesn't mean they're a bad person or that they don't love their partner. It's the boy's natural desire for new and exciting things that keeps him restless.

#7. General Characteristics:

- Personal enjoyment.
- Self-obsessed
- Loyal (but not with pleasure)
- Attention-Seeking
- Clingy
- Highly social
- Messy
- Bad at money management.
- Picky
- Fast-moving

- Active
- Acts like risk-taker but isn't. Scared of risks.
- Defensive
- Easily influenced by others
- Not honest with themselves
- Fast talker but doesn't think through.
- Not quick to lose temper but extreme when they do
- Always wanting to be something they aren't
- Loves electronics and anything new or up to date.
- Doesn't think before acting.
- Not good with routine.
- Not detailed-oriented.
- Intelligent and highly curious
- Lazy

#8. Teenage Boy Area

3	2	1
4	9	**8**
5	6	7

The area halfway to the back and on the right-hand side of any property or structure represents the teenage boy character. A teenage boy's life is full of change and excitement. It's the time when they're getting to know themselves and starting to think independently.

This is when teenage boys become more focused on the world and people around them. They also begin to develop a desire for external recognition. In many species, it can be seen that the teenage years are the years where boys establish their social ranking and try anything to test their limits.

This is why you'll often see teenage boys being so adventurous, looking for new ways to test their boundaries and show off their importance, power, and skill to others. One area where teenage boys excel is in competitive settings where they are able to win something by proving their skills and intellect. Sport is a good example of the kind of competitive environments teenage boys thrive in. Somewhere they can be both playfully competitive and highly social. They love being around a lot of people and want to be where the action is.

But, their competitiveness is also driven by a hidden lack of self-confidence. This is why they try so hard to hide anything about themselves which could be seen as weakness. Perhaps, this is why teenage boys feel such social pressure to prove themselves in front of their peers.

Consider the work style of a teenage boy for a moment. They'd excel at something like sales or customer service. They can talk to anyone, and enjoy challenges. But don't ask them to do anything that has to be done precisely or performed on a routine basis in isolation. They will get bored quickly and make mistakes. Their minds are just not focused on step-by-step details.

#8. Quick Example:

If someone's toilet is in this area, they will like to spend their money on trendy items that other people want to have. Most commonly, technology. They'll like to buy things other people can see so they can show off how "cool" they are.

#8. General Characteristics:

- Fashionable
- Up to date with trends
- Not confident
- Like challenges
- Does everything to look good/smart and confident
- Feel the need to "prove" themselves
- Unorganized
- Doesn't stay in one place for very long.
- Highly social
- Good with people
- Likes to try/learn new things
- Loves technology or gadgets.
- Doesn't think of others when talking
- Only thinks about the present moment
- Great talker
- Easy to influence others
- Risk-taking/
- Loves challenging themselves
- Follows others opinions
- Multi-tasking
- Acts without thinking
- Unique style and way of doing things
- Never plans ahead
- Thinks and acts fast.
- Adaptable
- Decisive

#9. Family Area

3	2	1
4	9	8
5	6	7

The family area is where it all comes together. It's beyond any single gender archetype. This is where blends it all together. If you consider a typical family unit, it's always dynamic. There's always something going on. Someone always seems to have a problem, and whatever is one's person's problem, becomes the whole family's problem. In a family unit, people share each other's emotions. If someone's sad, you're sad - if they're happy, you're happy. Individuals in this area are sensitive to others' feelings. But, it's ok because families always find a way to sort things out, no matter how bad it gets.

One of the great things about a family is how they support and share everything with each other. But, because people are so close, there are often tensions between people. Nothing is really private in a family. Family members try to hide their emotions from each other but cannot in the end. They always know what's going on with everyone else in the family.

The 9 area in a property or house has similar characteristics to this concept of a family. It's the place where everything comes together. It won't be used by only one person, always more than one. The 9 area is also a place where there will be problems and tensions between people (no matter what it's used for). But just as in any family, only one person will be the real head or leader in this area.

9. General Characteristics:

- Nothing is ever done alone
- Always helping other people or being helped
- Reckless
- Only ever used by multiple people at one time.
- There can only be 1 head or person in charge in this area
- Always has problems with others.
- No gray area. Everything good or bad.
- Emotionally sensitive
- Knows the value of things around.
- Acts as if they are confident leaders
- Want to be alone but can't.
- Feels lonely even when around a lot of friends
- Tries to hide their feelings from others
- Able to manage a lot of people
- Commanding
- Nosey, and wanting to know everything about others
- Great at organizing.

#9. Quick Example:

If a couple's bedroom is in the family area, only one of the two will be the head of the household and know everything that happens in that house. The other cannot be as influential or dominant as the other. It's difficult for people sleeping here to want sex.

CHAPTER 5
Recognizing The Areas

Now that we've covered what each area represents and how they influence people and their actions in those areas, we're able to move on to how to recognize where each zone is on a property. Once we have a better understanding of exactly how to divide up a house or office, we'll be able to connect them to the rooms in the house, giving us a complete picture of a person's life and lifestyle. Understanding where the character areas are, and how to connect them to a person's life can be simple, but not always easy. Let's go over the different factors to keep in mind when looking at the areas.

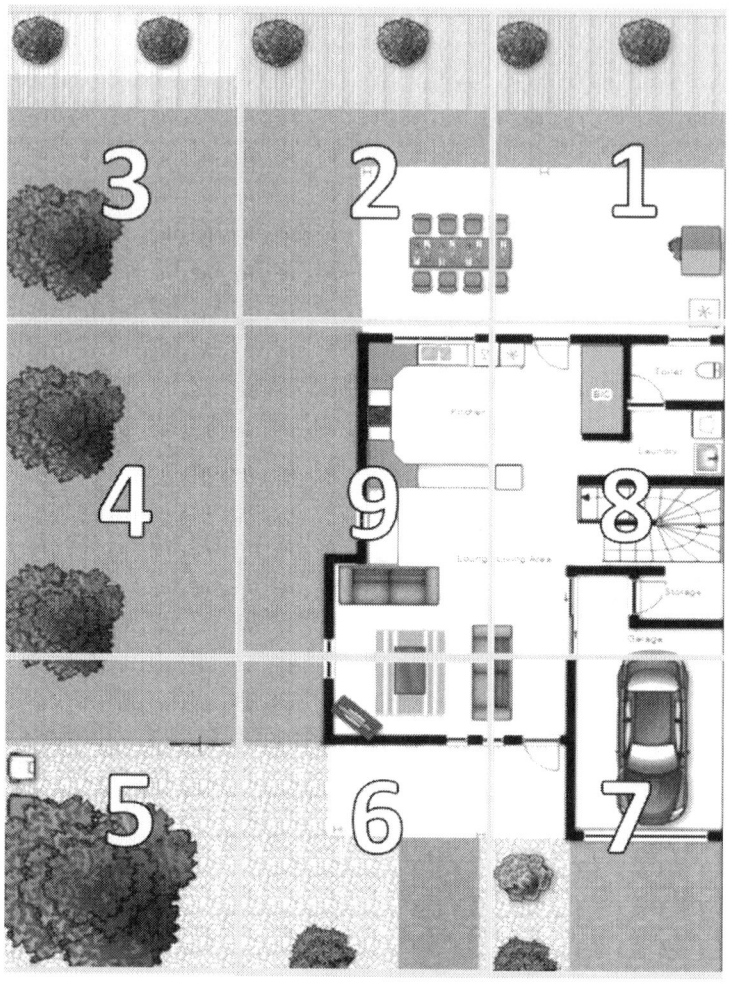

Perspective

Whenever looking at the areas of influence, we have to assume a birds-eye view perspective. We then place the bottom of the grid (5,6,7 areas) at the front of the property where the public road enters the private space of the property. If done right, the adult man area will be at the back right, and the adult woman will be at the back left, as seen on the previous page

If multiple roads are touching the property - like a corner lot - we look for the entrance to the property, according to its design. No matter how many roads lead to a property, there will always be a main entrance or gate by design of the property.

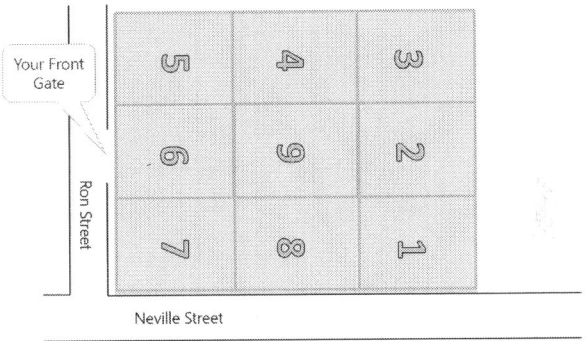

For example, in the image above, there are two streets adjacent to the property. Neville Street, and Ron Street. In this picture, the main entrance is on Ron Street. The grid will be aligned as shown, with the male zones closest to Neville Street.

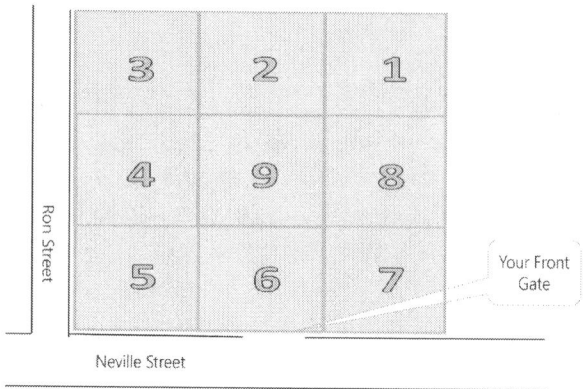

If instead, the entrance was by Neville Street, the grid would be as shown below, with the child areas now adjacent to Neville Street and the female areas closest to Ron Street.

Layers & Levels

Similar to our calendars, and idea of time, there are always multiple layers to everything. This applies to the areas of influence too. There isn't simply one grid for the entire property. There are layers of grids within grids, each showing us a different level of detail.

Wherever there are boundaries to a land area, such as created by a title or deed, an area of influence grid is created. We'll call this the land (L) grid. Then, somewhere on that plot of land, there will be a structure. Another grid is created for this area, the building (B) grid. Lastly, each room also has boundaries and therefore also creates a grid for the areas of influence, the room (R) grid.

Land Grid

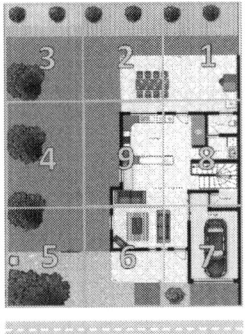

Building Grids

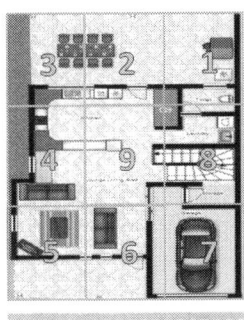

Room Grid

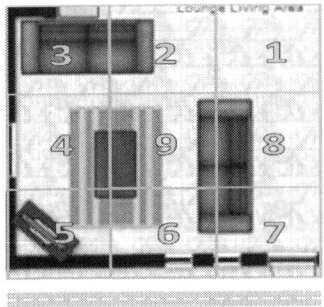

Combined Grids

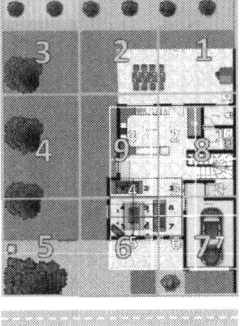

Each of these grids reveals something different about the people living or working there. If we look at the property as a whole, we discover their general personality plus broad influences affecting everyone in the house. At a land grid level, we look at where the structure is and the overall use of the property. For example, seeing the shape and position of the building on a property and the locations of external structures such as water tanks and swimming pools.

When looking at the building grid, a more detailed picture of each person's lifestyle is available. Here we are able to tell more about their habits and behaviors within the house. At the building grid level, the focus is predominately on the locations of the rooms, and their meaning in a person's life. The room grid reveals a person's interactions with specific objects within that particular room. You'll see how a person acts when in that room. At this level, we focus on the positioning of furniture and other items.

These grids are not separate from each other. In fact, they overlap each other. One affecting the other. This is something that makes each property and situation unique. The particular alignment allows advanced practitioners infinite levels of detail about a person's life and personality.

For example, the bedroom may be in the man area within the land grid while also in the young girl for the building grid, but with the actual bed could be located in the woman area of the room. Each grid tells a different part of the story.

This is a book for all levels of Feng Shui learners. We will focus on the primary areas for the sake of simplicity. Rather than going into detail by overlapping grids.

But, the longer you practice, the more of a person's life can be discerned. Given time, you'll be able to incorporate the multiple grids and know people's lives in increasingly greater detail.

You can even know whether someone separates their whites from colors when doing laundry, just from the position of their washing machine on their floor plan.

If you'd like to learn all of this is more intricate detail with live examples, keep an eye on Aur's website for any current Feng Shui courses available.

WHERE TO START

This depends on what we are looking for. If you'd simply like to gain an overview of a person's life and possible problems they may be experiencing, the best option is to first look at the land grid to see where the structure is. From here you can move deeper into their daily habits by looking at the building grid, and seeing where each room is in the house. This top-down approach will provide an overview of the inhabitant's personality, lifestyle, finances, relationships, and health.

Alternatively, we might want to answer a specific question about someone's life. For example, what their sleeping habits are. In this case, we'd identify what area of the house symbolizes their sleeping habits (the bedroom). Then we would look at where the bedroom was in the land and building grids to gain a detailed understanding of their personality and sleeping habits. Lastly, we would look at where the bed was in the room. This would give us precise details of that person's sleeping habits, possible health problems, and their relationships.

Soon we'll cover how to connect a person's actual behavior to the areas of influence, by looking at the symbolic meaning of each room in a structure. But, we first need address what makes every person, and house, unique. Where other Feng Shui styles like to generalize nature's influences on individuals, Aur focuses on how each case is unique. Only then can you understand the person and know how to improve their life, or your own, using Feng Shui.

CHAPTER 6
Basic Interferences

LET'S PAUSE FOR A MINUTE. Before we see what each room says about different areas of our life, we should first see what makes each of us different. No one person is the same, and neither are their preferences and needs in life. If two people lived in the same house but came from different backgrounds, worked in different industries, and were different ages, would we say the house influences them in the same ways? Not at all. Everyone is unique. We cannot apply Feng Shui principles without taking certain factors into account. Here are what we call the "basic interferences" when looking at any individual's home or workplace.

#1 Climate & Geography

Climate and geography affect the way in which we build our homes. In countries like Thailand and the Philippines, many houses are traditionally built on stilts, with large windows and [mostly] large open spaces. Thailand had frequent flooding and was often hot. The public areas and larger windows would allow air to flow around the house, providing cooler surroundings during the warmer seasons.

Whereas, in places like the Netherlands, houses are built close to the ground and often with smaller windows and small rooms. This is because the Netherlands and other Northern European countries endure long and cold winters. By keeping the rooms small, they are able to control heat within the house. Whereas, being on the ground provided the home the natural warmth.

These vast differences in temperature, climate, and geography change the way people live. In fact, entire cultures and religions were shaped by weather, seasons, and geography. Which brings us to interference number 2.

#2 Culture

Culture has vast implications on how people see themselves and others around them. It directs their moral compass and defines how they should live their lives. Life differs immensely depending on a person's upbringing. What is right in one region of the world won't be in another. In Thailand, it is common that whole families sleep together in one room. Most modern European and American families see it as the norm to have private areas for each family member. Therefore, we must take a person's culture into account when deciding what's best for them.

#3 Biological Gender

In reality, there is no gender. Each person's spirit, core personality, or however you may like to call it, is neither male nor female. However, the body we are born into has distinct gender influences. These biological differences create personality traits which change our interests and needs.

Chemistry within our body and brain influences our thoughts, relationships, and our views of the world around us.

Irrespective of whether a man has feminine qualities, they will still think, feel and act differently than a woman. He will demonstrate feminine aspects of his manhood. The same applies if a woman is confident, ambitious and independent. These are often associated with more masculine qualities. However, the way in which she expresses these qualities will still originate from her biological gender.

This is why analyzing the life of a man in the man area is different from that of a woman in the man area. Their biological sex creates different results in their final actions and feelings.

#4 Age

Would a child like to spend the whole day at a day spa? Probably not. Likewise, an adult wouldn't want to watch cartoons on repeat for 8 hours, either. They'd probably rather a trip to the dentist. Our personalities change a lot according to our age. As children, we're adventurers or dreamers. As teenagers, we start to find our identity and place in the world, testing our limits along the way. As adults, we look to create something for ourselves – be it a family, a successful career, or a sense of fulfillment in helping others. As we become older, we slow down and take more time to relax and enjoy more simple things. Age is a major factor when looking at Feng Shui.

If we are trying to see a person's sex life from their house and don't bear in mind that they are only two years old, or ninety-eight, we have certainly missed crucial details for consideration.

#5 Career

In Japanese, the term "Karoshi" translates to death from overworking. In Japan, over 10,000 people die at their desks each year due to overworking themselves. It isn't a surprise when you consider that they commonly work 60 to 70 hours per week.

This isn't usually seen in Western countries. But, it does demonstrate how large an impact our career has on our mind and body. Nearly twenty percent of an average person's life is spent at work, probably more if we include thinking about it. It's unrealistic to expect that it doesn't influence our personality. A fashion designer will have a very different lifestyle, thought process, preferences, and habits than an internal audit accountant. When looking at their work and living areas, we must keep in mind what they do and what it means.

Advanced Interferences

In the end, everything is connected. There are many factors which shape a person's life which we'll discuss in future books and courses. However, so you can at least know what they are, here are some advanced components which significantly change the way we interpret Feng Shui.

Advanced 1 - Date of birth

The day of the week a person is born directly impacts their personality, strengths & weaknesses, likes & dislikes. When fully understood one is able to know, not only a person's entire psyche just from this piece of information, but even make precise past, present, and future predictions of their life.

Society has forgotten why our ancestors created calendars with seven days in a week or that the days were originally named after planetary bodies (Sunday [Sun], Monday [Moon]). Our ancestors knew what they were doing.

Astrologers by nature, they knew that on each of the seven days, the planets and Earth would be differently aligned. This affected the natural elements on earth to change. Each day individual elements would be more dominant than others. It is this elemental imbalance that largely influences our personalities, health, and behavior, dependent on the day and time we're were born. This is why colors, numbers, names and basically everything influences each of us in different (but predictable) ways.

Advanced 2 - Property address

Everything in this world is connected to the natural elements. Even our numerical and alphabetical systems are symbols of the classical four elements. Every one of these symbols carries with it, the character of its associated element.

This is why every property, even with the same design and on the same street, is different. Because each property has its own elemental characteristics, they also affect each person differently. One house may help an individual born on a Sunday to be able to focus and think clearly while simultaneously resulting in anyone born on a Tuesday being sick or stressed. Every property affects people born on different days of the week, differently.

Advanced 3 - Colors

Although many Asian cultures have had long-standing beliefs around the different ways colors affect people, it is only recently that the West has started taking hues more seriously. People are becoming more aware of how to use color for design, marketing and psychology purposes. For example, therapists are using colors to reduce depression and anxiety in their patients. Whereas fast food chains are purposefully picking colors which create restlessness for their customers to get them in and out quickly. That's why nearly every one of them uses a combination of red and yellow.

On an individual level, most of us can feel that color affects us and will say for example that blue is a cooling and soothing color, whereas red is a warm or passionate color. In essence, each color is linked to a classical element, ranging from a red flame or a cold blue raindrop. But this also means that every color used in things around us influences that object and people's interactions with it.

The color people use in their homes and officers have a large effect on those occupying the space and their behavior. But, in which way, will depend on the address of the property and the person's birthday.

When combining all of these advanced interferences, we gain a much greater insight into a person's life. For example, red may be a good color for concentration in a house with the number 35.

If a Sunday child lives there, the child might be more selfish and stressed. Because people born Sunday are prone to pressuring themselves. For that reason, it may not be good to use red in the Sunday child's room.

PRE-CHAPTER 7
Rooms & Meanings

EACH ROOM IN IS CONNECTED to a different area of your life and reveals many details about a person. Just from a bedroom, we can see someone's sleeping patterns and how much time they spend in the room.

Our home also represents our minds so we can see something else from each room too. We can understand key aspects of their personality and lifestyle. From that same bedroom, we can tell someone's character while at home, their relationships with others in the house, and even their sexual style. This intrinsic meaning of each room is connected to our minds and the subconscious meaning we give each room. For example, the bedroom is the most private area for people. It's where they feel safe to be themselves. So it reflects their personality. When the bedroom is shared, it shows both their characters, which gives us an idea of their relationship. Each room is both a physical space in which we interact with the objects in the room, and symbolic of who we are, and our lives.

Over the following few chapters, we are going to go through each room of a typical house individually and how they directly influence and reveal our personalities and lifestyles. Each chapter starts with the meaning the room and what area of life the room represents. One by one, we connect the room with the 9 areas of influence, to see what it specifically means for that room to be in that particular area. Keep in mind that we are going to focus on the purest possible areas of influence and only looking at the property from the building grid only, for simplicity. In real-life, the meanings can and will be slightly (or vastly) different depending on the basic and advanced interferences, and the rooms' positions in relation to the land and building grids combined.

CHAPTER 7
The Bedroom
Life, Love, & Sex

THE BEDROOM IS A SANCTUARY. The one truly private space within the house. Especially if you live with others, or have kids. Although, if you have children, life is never private, not even for toilet breaks! For most, the bedroom is the place where you can really be yourself. And it should be – we spend nearly a third of our lives there.

The bedroom shows us who a person is and how they interact with others in the house. It also reflects the person's interactions with the bedroom itself. There are usually only a few activities we do in a bedroom, mainly sleeping and having sex. These are the two areas of a person's home life we can see from their bedroom.

If we want to know a person's personality, relationships, and bedtime habits, we can use the building grid and mentally lay it over the house as if viewed from above. As seen here. Remember to place the bottom of the grid on the wall closest to the main road, where the communal or government public area enters the private property.

Then we look at where the bedroom is positioned (in the picture above, it is in the #4 teenage girl area). Before reading into things we first we take into account the inhabitants' age, sex, culture, and career to form a picture of their core personality. This is important to know first if we want to have a clear under- 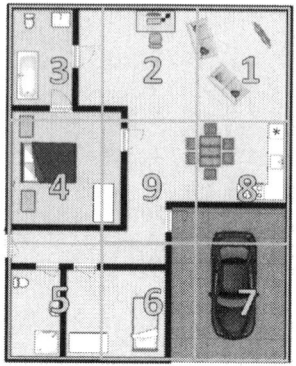 standing of the person sleeping there. A 5-year-old Japanese girl sleeping in the #1 man area will be very different than a 40-year-old male Brittish doctor. And when it comes to relationships, there's one more influence we need to consider.

What Side Do You Sleep On?

The side of the bed someone sleeps on affects that person's relationship with anyone they share the bed with. It isn't about who is right or left, but instead how the person is positioned within the areas of influence. When a couple shares a bed, generally the person closer to the back of the property will be in a higher position of power in their relationship. They'll be the one "wearing the pants." As you know, the front of the property is symbolic of a child, and the back is symbolic of the adult. Being further back is similar to being older and therefore someone who should be respected.

Let's say the darker figure in the image below represents the man, and the lighter, a woman. In regards to the couple sleeping in the top right #1 man area, the man will likely be the dominant of the two as he is further back than the woman. Whereas, take a look at the couple sleeping in the left #4. Area. You can see that the woman is "higher" or further towards the back of the building. This shows that she is the one who takes charge in the relationship.

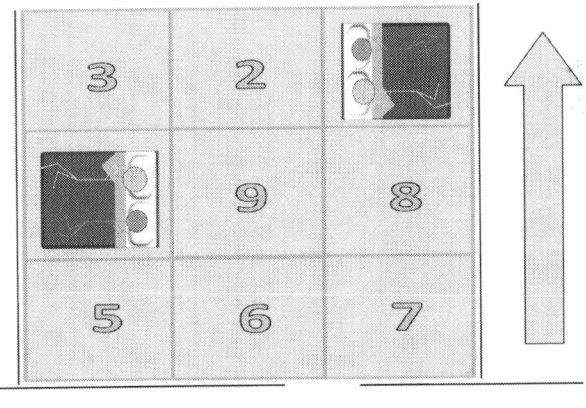

Note: *There are exceptions to this rule. For example, the day of the week each of them is born also affects their relationship. Some days naturally dominate over others. If a wife is born Sunday, but the man is born Friday, the wife will naturally be in charge. Also, being in charge doesn't mean being bossy. In some cases, it means the other takes care of everything in the house for them.*

#1. Bedroom In Man Area

3	2	🛏
4	9	8
5	6	7

Anyone sleeping in the adult man area will have masculine qualities as seen in an archetypical adult male. They'll be straightforward, spontaneous people who enjoy change. People sleeping here tend to focus on results and logic, rather than emotions. Being in the man area doesn't mean that a woman will start to enjoy football when she didn't before, nor will a child begin drinking beer.

These things are too specific. They aren't qualities every male has nor do they take the actual person into account. Whoever the person is, the existing areas of their personality which align with adult masculine qualities will be emphasized. The qualities will be ones seen predominantly in almost every male no matter their species, culture or creed.

We can assume that people with a bedroom in the man area like to stay in bed late and are deep sleepers, once they fall asleep. However these days it will be harder for them to actually fall asleep. They're quick thinkers, and able to make decisions quickly.

General Personality & Use of Room

- Confident
- Social and playful
- Deep sleeper
- Difficult to fall asleep
- Loves physical pleasures
- Not organized. But think they are.
- Feels in charge
- Feels responsible for others
- Results-driven
- More logical. Less emotional
- Thinks big picture
- Not detail-oriented
- Quickly bored
- Likes new things
- Likes to stay in their bedroom
- Loves many projects at once
- Single-minded
- Straight to the point
- Stubborn
- Focused
- Wants to remain in the room for a long time but can't.

Sex

Why should I snuggle? People sleeping here will generally see sex as a duty. They can be fun and adventurous once they get started, though. These people aren't afraid to be a little wild.

Just as for any man, done means done. They aren't the kind to linger. Their mind is focused only on one thing. When it's finished, they'll be thinking about what they are going to do next. Which is likely sleeping.

#2. Bedroom In 3rd-Sex Area

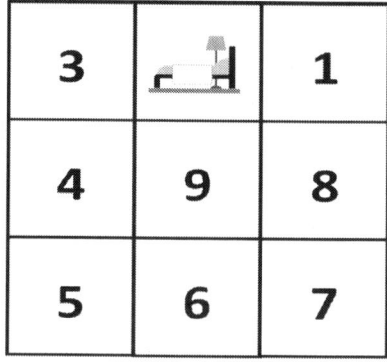

Someone sleeping in the 3rd-sex area of a house will have certain core similarities with those we associate with the universal idea of a third-sex character. In general, they'll be naturally creative people. But moody too. They are slow to trust other people and would rather not share much about their private life with others outside of their 'inner' circle. This may not be immediately apparent, though, because those sleeping here will seem outward, confident, and open about their lives. Although internally, they will have insecurities and keep many things private.

People sleeping in the 3rd-sex zone have a natural ability to think differently than most others and see the world from another perspective. They have both masculine qualities and feminine qualities and are often unpredictable as to which side they will show.

For the 3rd-sex personality, everything depends on how they feel at that moment. This is why people in this room won't go to bed at the same time each night. They also have a hard time making decisions and second-guess themselves, although they're still too stubborn to follow others. Think of it as "Even though I don't know what I want, I'm still not going to do what you want."

General Personality & Use of Room

- Goes to bed at a different time every night
- Everything based on mood
- Social on the surface
- Private about personal life.
- Only shows others what they want others to see
- Likes to be on their own
- Always thinks they're already perfect.
- stubborn
- Open minded & Empathetic to others.

- Difficulty making decisions Emotionally up & down
- Unsettled and restless
- Don't like change
- Think a lot
- Highly creative
- Dislike routine
- Attention-seeking

Sex

What am I in the mood for tonight? People sleeping in this room love new challenges in the bedroom but don't care if the sex is particularly good, or frequent. They'll only do something if they feel like it. The problem is that many times when one is in the mood, the other isn't. It's also hard changing someone's mind in this position. So, if tonight is not the night, it'll be hard to convince them otherwise.

#3. Bedroom In Woman Area

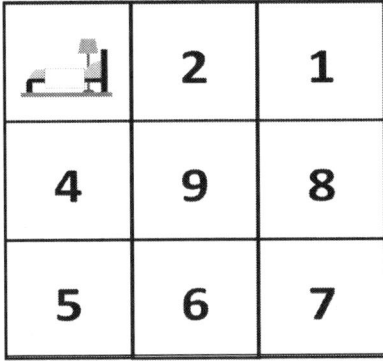

Anyone sleeping here will have more emphasized feminine qualities in their personality and behavior when at home. But don't think sleeping here will make a man start reading Cosmo and wearing heels. Only existing feminine qualities which are naturally part of their personality will be more pronounced. For example, a man will be gentler in character. They will be more romantic and sensitive. But they'll also become more talkative and nitpicky in this area. Whereas a woman will be even more detail-oriented and tend to nag more.

Universally, people sleeping in this area of the house will be detail-oriented, organized, and like to have everything in its place. They'll like to plan ahead, know everything going on around them, and what will happen next.

People sleeping here will have trouble getting to sleep. They've always got lots going on. Their minds will be active, and they'll be thinking about many things before going to sleep. People with a bedroom in this area tend to be light sleepers and easily woken by noises or movement around them. They're also unlikely to linger in bed once awake.

Appearances are paramount for anyone sleeping here. They like to take care of their "image," and worry about how others think of them. A bedroom in this area likely has various decorative objects in specifically chosen places.

General Personality & Use of Room

- Detail-oriented
- Highly organized
- Nags a lot
- (Sometimes too) Critical
- Romantic/Loves intimacy
- Likes personal surprises. (But not career or financial)
- Always thinks they are right
- Won't admit when wrong
- Emotionally driven
- Tend to be jealous
- Appearances are paramount
- Motherly
- Takes care of others
- Loves to plan ahead
- Patient, if they don't care about it. But if they want something, want it instantly

- Gets into other people's business even when nothing to do with them
- Deep sleeper but quickly awoken.
- Goes to bed late
- Wakes up early.

Sex

How about next Thursday at 8 pm? Adults sleeping here enjoy predictable routine. They love something they can count on. They feel like sex is a way of showing affection and that if they don't show affection regularly, something must be wrong in the relationship. They're likely to have a sexual 'routine' with their partner.

#4. Bedroom in Teenage Girl Area

3	2	1
🛏	9	8
5	6	7

A teenage girl goes through a lot of changes but isn't good at adapting to change. They are generally scared of it. Universal tendencies of a teenage girl that people will show if their bedroom is in this area will be qualities such as being generally quiet and keeping their private home life separate from their social life. They're the kind of people who thrive best when they have clear rules and structure in their lives. If you do get a glimpse into their bedroom, It'll most likely be messy. The bed can often end up looking more like a storage space, than a place to sleep.

People sleeping here think of what they'll get before they do anything. This means that they're often good in any area which requires doing things step-by-step, guided in routine, with a clear result at the end. For example, they have the ability to excel at anything with to do with books, academics, or paperwork. As long as it doesn't require any creativity. But, they'll only be good at it, if they consider it to be their responsibility. When they feel that something isn't their duty, they won't do it. People in the teenage girl area love keeping to themselves and won't often interact with others in the house. They love their family but don't feel the need to spend lots of time with them. However, when they are out, they're completely opposite. When out, they love to be around other people and stick close to their friends.

General Personality & Use of Room

- Private when at home

- Loves to be around people when out
- Clean, but untidy
- Complains about others
- Never blames themselves
- Likes others to do for them
- Not good with change
- Want change/scared of it.
- Good with routine duties
- Don't understand own feelings
- Insecure
- Lack confidence
- Jealous
- Love to gossip
- Not creative
- Excels at books, academics
- Keep home and social life separate
- Needs structure
- Does everything by "rules."
- Just gets things done
- Can be harsh with words
- Fights / Argues a lot

Sex

Can we just get it done? Someone whose bed is here will be insecure when it comes to their sexual abilities. They will more often than not let their partner do everything when they are together. They'll only care about themselves too when it comes to sex. So, when they're done, it's all over.

#5. Bedroom in the Young Girl Area

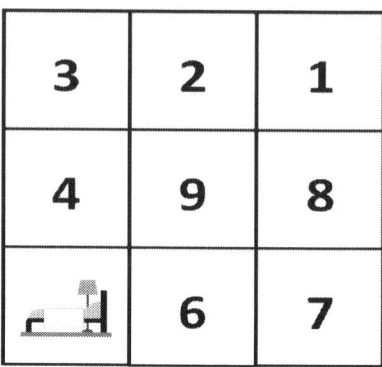

The young girl area is one of the three child areas. Kids generally don't like to stay in one spot all day, and neither do people whose bedrooms are in any three of these areas. Whoever sleeps here likes to spend time out of their bedroom, and are relatively active people.

Those who sleep in the young girl area don't tend to sleep well. They have over-active minds and often dream a lot, or lie in bed thinking too much. Out of all the areas in the house, this is the area which will most likely lead to sleep-talking. Their restlessness makes them wake up early too, generally leaving anyone who sleeps here feeling chronically unrested and tired.

A man sleeping in this area is different from a woman sleeping here. Typically, any man sleeping in this area will be a quiet and private person. Whereas a female sleeping in this position will love to be involved with whatever other people are doing and enjoy gossip. If a woman sleeps in this area of the house, she'll want to feel special, just like any young girl would. She'll be attention-seeking with those close to her.

General Personality & Use of Room

- Attention-seeking
- Talkative & likes to gossip
- Impulsive
- Loves affection
- Wants to look good
- Emotionally driven
- Highly imaginative
- Daydreamer
- Loves sweet behavior
- Active mind at night
- Doesn't sleep a lot
- Never thinks things through
- Dislikes being alone
- Bossy and critical of others.
- Blames others
- Light sleeper, never rested
- Only cares about looks

Sex

The first thought you may have is that it's wrong to think of a young girl's sexual preferences and that they shouldn't even exist. However, please remember that the young girl personality is simply the symbolic character of a universal natural force, not literally a young girl. These are character traits which can be seen in any person, no matter their gender or age.

Having said that, any man who sleeps in this area of a house won't have much interest in sex. A woman, won't want sex, per se, either. Instead, she'll want attention and affection from her partner, which could likely result in sex. But her primary motivator is that she wants her partner to make her feel special. That's why foreplay in this area will be good, but intercourse won't be anything special.

#6. Bedroom In Young 3rd Sex Area

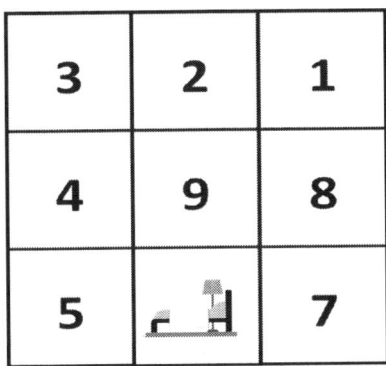

Those sleeping in the young 3rd-sex child area are generally withdrawn. They commonly lack confidence in whatever they do. They're often in their own world and feel forgotten by, or different from, others.

People here are usually happy to help those around them, and people around them often turn to people sleeping here whenever they have a problem. But, because this area is often seen as the "junk" area, they go unappreciated, even when they're valuable to others.

Just like other child positions, they are at the front of the house and won't be deep sleepers or the kind of people who stay in one place for long. This is partially explained by the natural, lasting, subtle vibrations within the earth caused by traffic movement, in combination with the road's influence on the earth's natural magnetic field. At a conscious level, this will go unnoticed. But their minds will be noticeably restless during the night, which will lead to poor quality of sleep.

General Personality & Use of Room

- Goes unnoticed
- Worries a lot
- Restless sleeper
- Not confident
- Feels unappreciated
- Does everything for those close to them
- Thinks differently than others around them
- Doesn't think much
- First person others go to when facing a problem
- Active, but not productive
- Happy to do things others don't want to do
- Not good at prioritizing
- Good with routine duties.
- This room generally isn't used often.

S<small>EX</small>

I can't do that, can I? It's pretty safe to say that no one's having sex here. They have too little self-confidence. On the off chance they do have sex, it won't be that good and likely to be over quickly. The good thing is that they'll do whatever they can to please the other.

#7. Bedroom In Young Boy Area

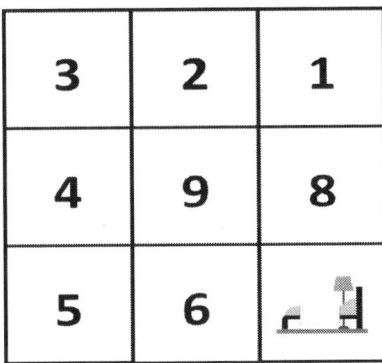

Young boys don't have time to sleep. There's too much to do. Too many games to play, or adventures to be had. Anyone sleeping in this position will be active and have lots of things going on in their lives. They can't sit still or simply do nothing. If they are sitting still, they're probably on their phone or computer, staying mentally active in one way or another.

People living here won't sleep much. They'll have a hard time getting back to sleep once they wake up too. Generally, people sleeping in the young boy area won't spend much time in their bedroom. They'll rather be out and about, often doing something socially with friends. If they're not out, they'll be on the internet or phone.

People here love everything "new." Similarly to how young boys love change and to experience new things. Anyone sleeping in this area will get bored quickly, and be terrible with details. Although they won't like to admit it, their lives will actually be relatively routine. This is a good place to sleep for those working weekday jobs where they need to wake up and get out of the house early each day.

If you've ever asked a young boy to clean something, you'll know two things. Firstly, being tidy and organized is not in their nature, and secondly, even if they do clean something, it still won't be done 100% accurately. Anyone sleeping here will be the same. They won't bother with details, and what they believe to be their best, will still be full of mistakes. After all, they're boys, and boys want to explore the world, not spend their time checking for errors.

General Personality & Use of Room

- Hates routine/
- Has a routine life
- Loves to be active but lazy.
- Very playful
- In their own world
- Doesn't think about others
- Loves to meet new people
- Messy
- Doesn't think much
- Does whatever they want
- Full of desire
- Loves adventure
- Loves being carefree

- Doesn't sleep much
- Wakes up early
- Loves anything new
- Makes mistakes
- Careless

Sex

Couples beware! A person in this position will get bored quickly. If a couple sleeps here, there's an 80% chance the man will become restless and want to have other partners. On the other hand, a woman sleeping in this area won't be that interested in sex. She'll be too busy with other areas of her life.

#8. Bedroom In Teenage Boy Area

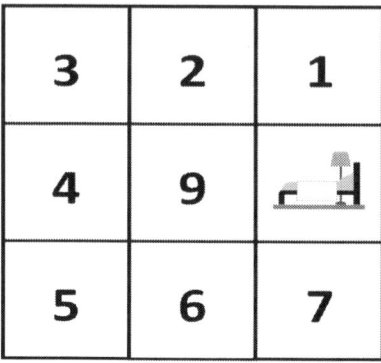

Teenage boys like new and exciting things, similarly to their younger counterparts. But, teenage boys are more social and like to test their boundaries too. Teenage boys enjoy finding ways to compete with each other and prove their power. They love showing off their skills for attention. They're naturally boisterous. Similarly, the person sleeping here will be social, cheeky, and playful. They'll hardly spend any time in the bedroom unless they're playing computer games or something similar.

You can tell that they love being around other people. Teenage boys seem to be natural networkers. On the other hand, anyone here will despise paperwork and anything that has to be done in a routine or structured manner. They like to do things their way, and only do the things they want to do.

The problem for people sleeping here is that they'll wake up at weird times, for no apparent reason. People sleeping here tend to be nighttime people rather than morning people. They like to sleep in but are quick to get ready when they have to leave.

General Personality & Use of Room

- Social
- Playful
- Cheeky & Mischievous
- Likes to show off
- Wants to prove himself
- Feels the need for acceptance from others
- Likes excitement
- Tidy, but never cleans
- Doesn't show their emotions
- Loves to network
- Hates paperwork or routine
- Loves everything up to date
- Wakes up weird times
- Doesn't stay in the bedroom
- Fast thinker
- Most likely to be up to date with trends and news.

Sex

Where's the fun at? People in the teenage boy area like to keep things fresh. If you want to try something new, they're up for it. Ideal for new couples. But, for long-term relationships, it'll just be "do it, and get it done."

Naughty secret: Out of all the areas to sleep in, this one is most likely to have an adult toy collection.

#9. Bedroom In Family Area

3	2	1
4	🛏	8
5	6	7

This is a unique area. Whoever sleeps here, is at the center of it all. They want to be alone. But, they can't do anything by themselves. Because this area represents a family, everything comes together here (including problems). It can be hard for some to sleep here. They'll have so much going on in their lives involving many people.

Anyone sleeping in this position will put themselves into everyone else's affairs in the house. There is nothing that happens in the house that they don't know. They're the first person everyone goes to with their problems too. This can be a tough area to sleep for some. They attract all the good things to them, but all the bad too.

If a couple sleeps in this area, only one of them will be in charge. Similarly to having the head of a family, there is one individual who has influence over others in the household. In many relationships (particularly in western culture) both the man and woman are of equal standing – this won't be the case for those sleeping here.

General Personality

- Knows everything that happens in the house
- Involved in everyone's affairs in the house
- If strong-minded will command everyone in the house.
- If a weaker-minded person, everyone in the house will control them.
- There's always a problem in this person's life.
- Never does anything alone.
- Doesn't like to sleep alone.
- Only one can be in power
- Takes on others' problems as their own.
- Commanding, but always with reason

*SPECIAL MENTION

If a father of the household is the dominant one in this position, he'll be commanding, and want to know everything about everyone's life in the house.

If the mother is the dominant one, her daughters won't marry. Instead, they'll likely be like "old maids." Even if they marry, they'll divorce because their mother is so commanding and needy.

SEX

Sex? Not here. It's unlikely the people here will want to have sex. If it does happen, it'll have to start in a different room first and then continue here.

Bedroom Tips

When it comes to authentic bedroom Feng Shui, every house is unique. Factors such as room and furniture colors, the inhabitants' birthdays and the relative position of the bedroom and structure on the property all change what we can tell about a person's life from their bedroom Feng Shui.

But, there are some "rules" in life which we can generalize. The sun will rise, the taxman will come, and the last bite of an ice cream will make you remember the first bite, and how fast it disappeared (or is that just me?). In this section, we'll look at good tips for good Feng Shui in any bedroom.

Parallelism

There are many forces of influence around us at all times, impacting our minds, health, and behavior. Of these, magnetic fields and seismic activity are particularly consequential. A significant source of magnetic and vibrational energy comes from the road in front of our home. Each road carries subtle vibrations, caused by the movement of cars, even after they've long passed. The movement also affects wind patterns and the earth's magnetic fields. Which in turn, influence our body and mind.

When we sleep, our bodies release electromagnetic energy and heat. The majority of which emanates from our heads and feet. But, when a bed's head is facing the road, the subtle energies emitted from the road interacts and directly collides with those from our head. This commonly leads to frequent headaches, shoulder and neck problems, accompanied by poor quality of sleep.

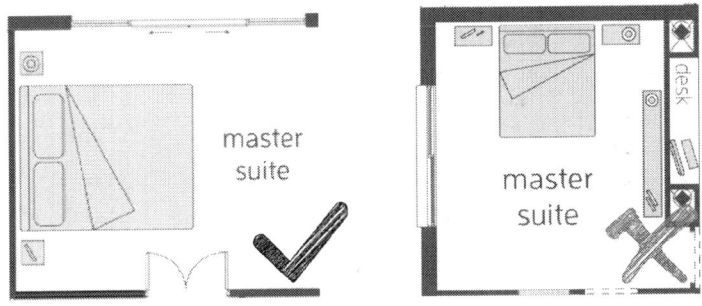

When the foot of a bed faces the road, the energies collide too, forcing the electromagnetic energy back into the individual's lower body. People with their bed's foot facing the road, will (over time) suffer from problems with their lower joints and knees. They're likely clumsy, often injuring their lower body.

When a bed is parallel to the road, the magnetic and vibrational forces don't directly collide with the major "outlets" from the body. Therefore, a person's health will be better over the long term if their bed is parallel to the road.

Electronics

All electronic appliances and equipment emit electromagnetic energy. A TV, even when turned off, is continuously emitting electromagnetic energy. See it for yourself. Touch the screen. Even when off, you can still feel static electricity emanating from it.

Many people like to have a TV at the foot of their bed. But this isn't good for your health. Similarly to when the bed's foot is facing the road, if the foot of the bed is directed to a television or other electrical appliance, it'll be harmful to the person's health (over time) – especially their nervous system.

A TV at the end of the bed results in nerve problems with the feet, knees, and lower back, over time. Whereas, if the electrical device or appliance is at the person's head, they'll have problems with concentration, sleep quality, and suffer neck and shoulders cramps.

From a purely muscular perspective, if a person has a TV at the end of their bed and spends time watching it, they will experience long-term damage to their neck and shoulders. Although this depends on how they sit or lie down to watch TV.

Note: Because of the metallic backing providing their reflective surface, mirrors have adverse health effects similar to electrical devices. They return the electricity to the sleeping individual and should never be kept at the foot or head of the bed.

AIRCONDITIONERS & FANS

Most people (especially in hotter climates) sleep with a fan or air conditioner in their bedroom. It's a part of modern life and provides comfort for deep, restful, sleep. However, they can be harmful. If the air from either flows directly towards a person's head or feet while they sleep, it'll lower the temperature in those areas, driving away blood and warmth. A lack of blood flow and fresh oxygen to the brain and feet can have serious health repercussions.

Many people with air conditioners at the head of their bed, which blows down onto them, often experience a mental blurriness. They'll have a hard time concentrating and feel drowsy and slow in the morning. This is because the cold air causes a lack of fresh blood and oxygen to the brain. Similarly, if a fan or air conditioner is facing a person's feet, the lack of oxygen and blood will cause long-term numbness, pain, muscle cramps and tingling in their feet and lower legs. It's better to have cool airflow coming from the side.

BOOKS & BEARS

People love books. Some even keep small libraries of them in their bedroom. Most children love having teddies and stuffed animals. But, both books and teddies can slowly drain our energy and health.

We all know that dust collects everywhere around us. Carried in by the wind, or produced from our own shredded skin cells and dust mite castings. Dust is made of many substances. If it collects to high enough levels, it causes health problems. In the short term, dust ignites allergy symptoms and weakens the immune system. In the long run, exposure to dust leads to lower lung efficiency and potential heart problems.

Books and stuffed toys collect lots of dust. If books or toys are kept in the bedroom, it'll cause health problems for those sleeping there. One book or teddy isn't likely to result in problems, but if you're a serious collector, it's best to keep your library and cuddle collection in a different room.

Water

When I was young, I had an aquarium in my room. Many people like the sound of water and buy water features or small aquariums for their bedroom. Popular Feng Shui "Masters" go so far as to suggest it for prosperity.

But in fact, any artificial body of water becomes a breeding ground for bacteria and viruses. You can see this for yourself when looking at a fountain or aquarium that slowly becomes green. Keeping water such as a fountain or water feature anywhere in the house results in problems. As the water naturally evaporates, it also spreads the pollutants carried inside which mix with the air we breathe.

Inhaling a constant bombardment of germs like this taxes the immune system which causes the body and mind to become irritated This leads people in the house to become more frequently sick, moody, and argumentative.

RELIGIOUS IMAGES

Although uncommon, some people do love to have religious figures or images in their bedroom. They may have a little Buddha or a Christian cross. Whatever they're religion, this subconsciously disrupts our sex lives. Subconsciously, we don't want to be intimate in front of a smiling Buddha or a Jesus on the cross (or any other deity or religious symbol). Having them there just doesn't help us to relax or be our best sexual selves.

If you want to have fun and adventurous romance in your bedroom, keep religion out of it. Let the religious figurines stay in your living room, or anywhere you don't plan to have adult time.

Bedroom Practice #1
Fred's Bedroom

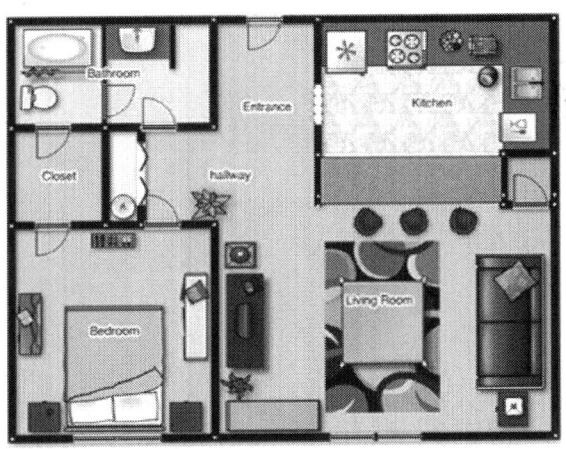

Using what we have just learned about the bedroom, try and practice by looking at the floorplan above and "predicting" the person's life and habits.

This is Fred's house. Fred is a single 20-year-old student, living in a one bedroom apartment in Amsterdam. By looking at the space, what can we say about Fred's personality and his lifestyle? First, when reading an individual's floorplan, we must find out where the public road is. In this case, Fred has told us that the main entrance where the property connects with the road, is on the side where his bedroom and living room are. Next, we would generally look at the entire land area to first find out where the house, room, and bed are in relation to the land, building and room grids. But, for the sake of simplicity, let's purely focus on Fred's floorplan. What area of influence is his bedroom in? Using the property grid, we can tell that his room is in the "Young Girl" area.

What can we say about Fred's personality? We can see that Fred is an active person. He doesn't sleep a lot. But, he will also likely suffer from health issues such as headaches or shoulder and neck pains. This is because his bed's head is facing the road. Fred won't like to spend time in his room. He's also likely to be a quiet person.

CHAPTER 8
Bathroom & Toilet

Money Habits

Let's move on to the bathroom. Traditionally, water has always been associated with money. Water is the most primal resource when it comes to life and death. Our ancestor's survival came down to how much water they had access to, and how they managed the precious resource. In today's society, it's the flow of money which determines whether a person survives or thrives. In our minds, money is today's life source. However, the underlying relationship between humans and water has never fundamentally changed. Although often underappreciated, water is still our most prized resource. It's our own perceptions about money which creates the correlation between the two.

Today, the place where the most water leaves the house is the bathroom. This is why it's the bathroom that represents how a person spends money. The most important aspect of a bathroom is the toilet. It reveals how they spend money.

After reading this chapter, you'll know whether someone spends their money on little things or big things, useful things or trendy nonsense, just from their toilet. Also, you'll be able to see whether they can keep money at the end of each month, or if it all goes down the drain. This is why we will focus specifically on the toilet.

Before we start, keep in mind that each toilet in a building will only represent the spending habits of those who use that bathroom. If one member of the family uses one bathroom, and the other uses another, each person's individual spending habits will be represented by the particular bathroom they use.

Alternatively, if a bathroom is mostly used by guests and or visitors, it will show how the inhabitants spend their money on social outings on other people.

Important!

Whether a person makes $1 or $1,000,000, <u>if their toilet is facing the wrong way</u>, they'll find themselves living month to month, with little left at the end.

It's important to mention that the direction of a toilet has a significant impact on the way a person spends money. When looking at a house, the toilet's direction reveals whether a person spends all of their money each month, or has something to save at the end of the pay cycle. It's quite simple. When looking at any house from a bird's eye view, we can tell if a toilet is either perpendicular to the road or parallel to it (rarely do you see a toilet that is diagonal.).

99% of the time, if the toilet is perpendicular to the road, people using that toilet will go through all of their income each month. They'll have little to nothing left by the end of each pay cycle.

Whereas, if the toilet is parallel to the road, they'll be more in control of their finances and able to keep money at the end of each month.

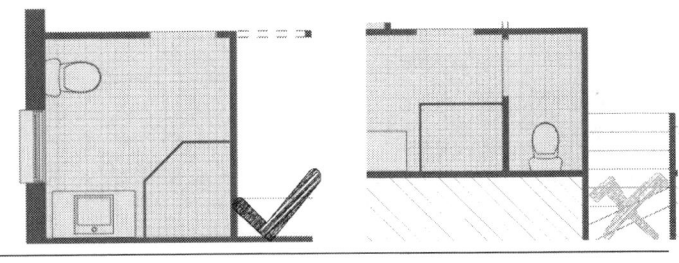

See the image above. Imagine the double lines represent the front road. The toilet on the right indicates that the user will go through their resources every month. On the other hand, the toilet on the left signals that the user is able to control their expenses every month. They're likely to have resources left.

Don't worry if your toilet is facing the wrong way, though. There is a way to fix a toilet facing the wrong direction without ripping out the plumbing. We'll soon get to that. But first keep in mind that spending a lot of money isn't a bad thing for everyone. It can be a good thing too.

For many shops owners, spending money each month often means they're replacing sold stock. This points to revenue coming in too. Also, shop owners don't usually keep money on the premises. So having a toilet facing the "wrong" way in their shop could be a sign of good business.

Another example would be a hotel owner. Hotel owners typically love it when their guest's toilets are perpendicular to the road. That way their guests are likely to spend more during their stay.

In case you're not a shop owner or a hotel chain, here's the way to fix your toilet. If your toilet is perpendicular (facing to *or* away from), you can use a U-shaped carpet or mat to mitigate the adverse effects. See below.

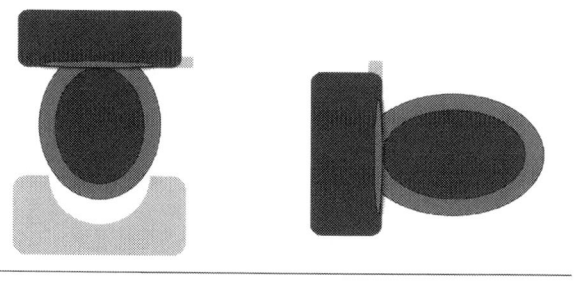

NOTE: *DO NOT put a U-shaped mat under an already parallel positioned toilet. It'll cause you to spend money as if your toilet was facing the wrong way.*

One key here is the color of the mat you choose. The color will affect your finances and the people in the house. Which colors are right and wrong for a house depends on many factors and differ for each property. Unfortunately, we aren't able to go into colors in this book as it's a whole topic on its own.

If you do need to buy a toilet mat for your toilet and would like to be sure to pick the right color for your house, we suggest getting in touch with us via our website.

#1. Toilet In Man Area

3	2	🚽
4	9	8
5	6	7

Knowing the toilet is connected to money, think for a moment, how does a man spend money? Does he buy little things or big things? Is he attracted to a "sale" sign? Not really. Does he buy things to make himself feel good about himself? Not quite.

The average guy isn't interested in small purchases or sales items. Instead, he usually has his eye on large, flashy things. Men want big boy toys, like a new car, big screen TV, or a new surround sound system. Whatever it is, they like to have the best of the best, of that thing. Men don't like poor quality. They like to have things they can show off. The main point is, when a man buys something, he buys big, and he buys the best. He doesn't care that much about price, but rather how good it is (only according to this own mind).

Anyone using a toilet in the man area will be the same. They won't care too much about price tags when they go shopping. They'll like to buy big, buy whatever they want, and buy something that can show off their status.

#1. Key Spending Habits

- Uses money in large amounts
- Buys new and up-to-date items
- Always wants the best or highest quality
- Doesn't care about price tags.
- Shows off how much they have with the items they buy.

#1. Key Bathroom Habits

- Spends a lot of time in the bathroom.
- Likes to read, play games, check emails or sit and think while in the bathroom.
- Won't keep the bathroom tidy, but it will be clean.

Special Note: Guest Bathroom

If the guest bathroom is in the man position, people living here will spend a lot of money on their social life. When they go out, they'll like to make it a big occasion. They don't mind paying for friends.

#2. Toilet In 3rd-Sex Area

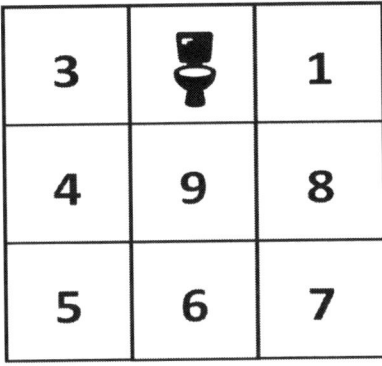

The uniqueness of the 3rd-sex adult leads them to like different things than most others. When a 3rd-sex adult buys something, other people won't understand why they would choose such a thing. 9-inch leopard print stiletto disco heels? Fabulous. But certainly not every man's style. The 3rd-sex adult has their own way of seeing the world, which is evident in their spending habits. People with a bathroom in this area love to spend time in there. But when they do, others will have no idea what they're up to in there. It's like they have their own little world inside that room. They like everything clean and tidy but are usually too lazy to do it themselves.

#2. Key Spending Habits

- Others don't agree with or understand, the ways they like to spend money their money.
- Are indecisive when shopping.
- When they like something, they'll buy a lot of it.

- Buys things that make them feel good
- Only buys things they believe are a reflection of their personality.
- Shops to cheer themselves up

#2. Key Bathroom Habits

- Spends a lot of time in the bathroom
- No one knows what they do in there.
- Likes to have a clean bathroom.
- Doesn't usually clean it themselves.

#3. Toilet In Woman Area

🚽	2	1
4	9	8
5	6	7

When a bathroom is in the woman's area, we know with certainty the bathroom will be clean, and whoever uses that bathroom likes to have everything in its place. Be careful! If you move anything in there, they'll know. Everything is exactly where it is for a (their) reason. Women spend a lot of time in the bathroom, but they don't hang out in there like a man does. You won't find a woman sitting on the toilet reading a novel. When they are done doing what they needed to do, they'll tidy up and leave.

If you look at the way a woman spends her money, you can see that women don't usually spend money on big items, like new cars or big screen TVs. Instead, women tend to spend money on lots of little things, until their money is all gone. Especially if those little things are on sale. A woman's logic dictates that saving money means to spend a hundred dollars on something which was originally two hundred. Regardless of whether she actually needed it or not. Those with a toilet in this area like to spend money on other people, especially their spouse or family. The problem is that they don't realize how much they've used until it's all added up in the end.

#3. Key Spending Habits

- Will buy anything "on sale."
- Buys mostly small items.
- Buys things for the house and others.
- Never buys just one item. Always comes home with multiple things.
- People with a bathroom here probably have a nicely decorated house. They like knick-knacks.

#3. Key Bathroom Habits

- Will use the bathroom often but won't linger.
- The bathroom will be immaculate.
- Everything is in its special place.

Special Note: Guest Bathroom

If this is a guest's toilet, it reveals that this person often spends money on social occasions out of a sense of duty or necessity. They may believe that they <u>must</u> see their friends. Or that they have to visit their family, for whatever reason.

#4. Toilet In Teenage Girl Area

3	2	1
🚽	9	8
5	6	7

In movies, we always see teenage girls in malls, and in love with fashion. But what are their motivations behind spending money? Teenage girls only ever buy things when they're are with their friends. They love being around others. For them, shopping is a social experience, rather than a chore. They buy things, not because they need them, but because it makes them feel good to do it. If they think something is cute, or that it will make them feel self-confident, they will buy it. Even if they never plan to use it.

What about their bathroom habits? Anyone who has lived with a teenage girl knows that they leave everything lying around in a seemingly chaotic mess in their bathroom. But, if you dare touch anything, they'll have the uncanny ability to notice any slight changes to their chaotic order. People in this bathroom are more likely to spend time making themselves look good, rather than using the room for personal hygiene.

#4. KEY SPENDING HABITS

- Spends money on trendy things.
- When friends buy something, they feel like they have to have it too.
- Spends money on anything a woman likes to buy, including fashion, makeup, accessories.
- Emotionally driven.
- Buys things they may never even use.
- Never shops alone. Loves to be with others.

#4. KEY BATHROOM HABITS

- Never tidy, but feels that everything's in its place.
- Will know if anything has been moved or taken from that room.
- Spends time making themselves look good.
- Doesn't spend much time in the shower or on the toilet.

#5. Toilet In Young Girl's Area

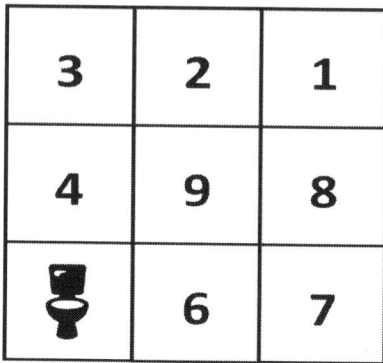

What do young girls love to buy? What's their primary motivation when deciding on what to get? Easy. They like cute things. Think of Barbie's, teddies, tea sets, decorative knick knacks, dolls, or tiaras.

This doesn't mean that everyone with a bathroom in the young girl area will want to buy a dollhouse. But, it does mean that EVERYTHING they buy, has an emotional or sentimental reason behind it, not a practical one. They simply don't think whether the things they buy are useful or not. That's not the point. For them, the whole purpose of buying something is to make them feel good.

If someone's bathroom is in this area, it'll always be hygienically clean, but almost certainly be messy. These people don't spend much time in the bathroom anyway.

#5. Key Spending Habits

- Love spending money on little things
- Don't think when they buy something
- Always buying things for their appearance.
- There's always something wrong with whatever they choose to buy.
- Buys anything that makes them feel special.

#5. Key Bathroom Habits

- The bathroom is clean but untidy.
- Don't spend time in the bathroom
- Don't think while in there.

#5. Special Note: Guest Bathroom

If a guest's bathroom is in this area, people living here will only spend money on those close to them, but won't think first before buying things for them. They'll also be very cautious when it comes to new people in their lives.

#6. Toilet In Young 3ʳᵈ-Sex Area

3	2	1
4	9	8
5	🚽	7

A person whose bathroom is in the young 3rd-sex area will hardly spend any time at all in there. They simply do what they need to do, and leave. Unlike, someone who has a bathroom in the man area, who could stay in there all day (if there were a fridge and TV). Like anything else in the 3rd sex area, the bathroom won't often be used.

Similar to that of the adult 3rd-sex, people with a bathroom in this area would have different shopping motivations than most others. The way they spend their money is in fact so different, that other people wouldn't ever think of buying the things these people buy. Nor would they want to.

Others will generally think that the way those with a young 3-rd sex toilet spend their money doesn't make sense. They'll feel that it's a waste to buy the things these people like. That's probably (at least part of the reason) why those with a bathroom in this area, don't like to talk about money. They're generally private about their finances.

#6. Key Spending Habits

- Buys things others would never have thought of.
- Always buys things that they have to personalize or modify to make their own.
- Can't make decisions on what to buy
- Selfish. Only ever spends money on themselves.
- Buys things they like even if everyone says it's stupid.
- Don't like people to know how much money they have.

#6. Key Bathroomhabits

- The bathroom won't get used much.
- People won't think to clean this bathroom.
- This bathroom is often forgotten.

#7. The Toilet In Young Boy's Area

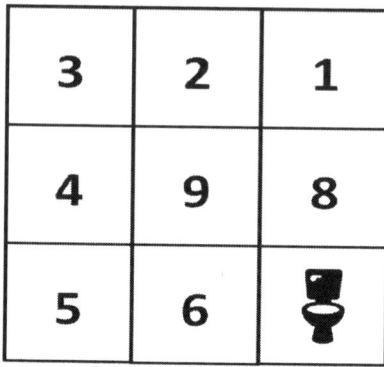

Who would you least likely want to give your credit card to? A little girl, or a little boy? Probably neither. But the boy's problem is that, if given free rein, he'll want everything in sight. His desires are endless. A young boy likes to have everything that looks new and fun. You can expect him to always want the latest gizmos, gadgets, phones, computers, and toys. But, it has to be brand new. And, it has to be available right now. Because a boy only ever thinks in the present moment. Current actions which will create problems in the future? A young boy doesn't reflect on these things. So, guess what group of people is most likely to be in debt? That's right, those with a bathroom in the young boy area.

What about their behavior in the bathroom? Young males don't usually spend much time in the bathroom. They lead active lives and would rather be doing something more interesting that sitting on the toilet. But, they're also forgetful and lazy. They probably won't clean or tidy up after themselves. They're the most likely out of all the different characters to forget things like turning off the lights, or flushing.

Those with bathrooms are in this area of the house will have many similar traits to those of a young boy when it comes to spending money and using the bathroom.

#7. KEY SPENDING HABITS

- Likely to get into debt
- Spontaneous when shopping.
- Often buy things they never actually use.
- Get bored quickly with the things they have.
- Always want something they don't yet have.

#7 KEY BATHROOM HABITS

- Don't like spending time in the bathroom.
- In and out.
- Not tidy, not clean.
- Careless, often forgetting the light or to flush.

SPECIAL NOTE: GUEST BATHROOM

If this is a guest bathroom, the person or people living there will love socializing and spending money on their friends. They enjoy any activities with their buddies. Like going out to dinner or enjoying other social experiences together.

#8. The Toilet In Teenage Boy Area

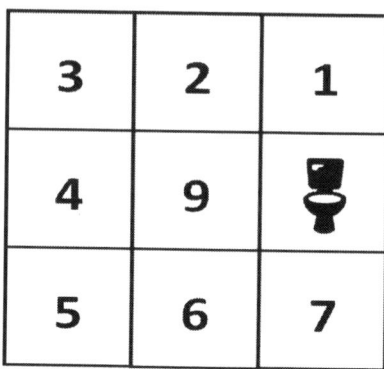

One of the primary goals of a teenage boy's life is to achieve social status. Just like any social animal, humans organize themselves into hierarchies, and the teenage boy's role is to find his position in his pack, (preferably at or near the top).

To get there, he needs the latest gadgets, toys and anything other people may look up to or envy. He loves to impress others or show everyone that he is important. The same goes for the spending habits of those with a toilet in this area of the house.

As for their time in the bathroom, they don't like spending much time in there. These people are usually too busy to be there for that long. They'll keep up appearances and make sure that everything is tidy, but it's unlikely to get cleaned often.

#8. Key Spending Habits

- Buys things to impress others.
- Uses their money to show off.
- Always buys according to latest trends (the newest smartphones, or this season's fashion).
- Loves to buy technological things and gizmos.
- Buys what they think is fun.
- Spends money on entertainment.

#8. Key Bathroom Habits

- Doesn't spend much time in the bathroom.
- Tidy but not often cleaned.

#9. The Toilet In Family Area

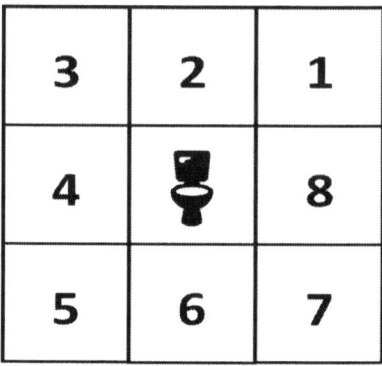

A family is never just one person. But, this doesn't mean everyone has to go to the bathroom together. Having a toilet or bathroom in this area means people living here will always spend money on other people. For example, buying things for the family as a whole. Or, helping relatives financially each month. Those with a bathroom in the family area will often think of others in their family when shopping. When they go to the supermarket or mall, they'll notice items their son or mother or husband may like and buy it for them.

They'll use the bathroom frequently, but never for an extended period of time. People with a toilet here don't like the isolation of being in the bathroom by themselves. If they're in there a long time, they're likely on their phones or tablets. The bathroom will probably be a mess too because nobody wants to clean up after someone else. Everyone uses the bathroom, but no one wants to pick up the sponge.

#9. Key Spending Habits

- Always spending money on other people.
- Gives money to family or pays for them.
- Whenever they get money, they use it right away.
- Their spending habits are a mix of everything. One day they'll buy big, the next small, the next can't decide, the next spontaneous and so on.
- Spending habits change day by day.

#9. Key Bathroom Habits

- Used often by everyone in the house.
- Won't stay in there long. Don't like being alone.
- Messy, but no one wants to clean it.

Potty Practice 2.
Fred's Bathroom

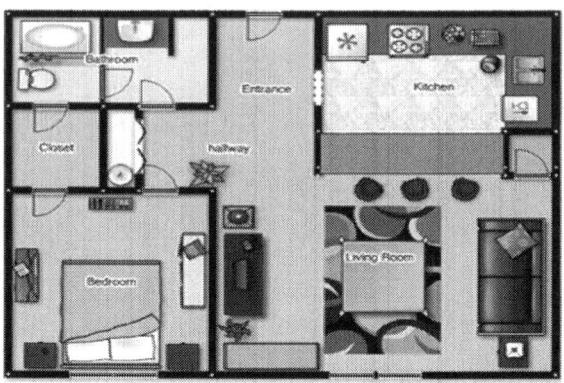

Let's look at Fred's apartment again. We already know that he doesn't spend much time at home and that he's a quiet but emotionally-motivated individual from his bedroom.

But, what can we say about his spending habits? For this, we'd take a look at his bathroom, especially the toilet. When looking at the bathroom, the first thing we check is the direction of the toilet. Is it facing towards or away from the road? Or, is it parallel to the road? We can see here from Fred's floor plan that his toilet runs parallel to the road. This is good for Fred. It means that he is able to manage his money and doesn't waste it all each month.

Next, what area of the building is it in? It's in the far left corner, which is the adult woman's area of influence. In that case, Fred would spend the majority of his money on little, routine things throughout the month. Most likely something to do with duty, such as bills and other financial commitments.

Also, we can tell from his floor plan that he likes to keep his bathroom clean and tidy, but wouldn't likely spend a lot of time in there doing something other than what the room is meant for.

CHAPTER 9
Kitchen & Dining Room

Family Life

THE KITCHEN IS the one room in the house where the whole family comes together. This is where everyone in the home interacts with each other to share their stories and lives with each other. It should come as no surprise that the kitchen shows a lot about family relationships in the house.

In some houses, the dining room and kitchen are separate. If so, we can tell how people interact with each other while eating and their eating habits, from the dining room. Do they eat together, every night at the same time? Or is it a grab and go kind of family?

Whereas the kitchen reveals how they cook and prepare meals. You can even tell how food will taste depending on where the kitchen is in the house. This counts for restaurants too. By the end of this chapter, we'll include tips on how to pick the best restaurant every time, just from the position of the kitchen. But first, let's look at what we can tell about a person's life from their kitchen at home, depending on which area of influence it is within the house.

#1. Kitchen In Man Area

3	2	🍽
4	9	8
5	6	7

You can immediately tell that a family who eats in this area is close. If you walked in as they were having dinner, you'd straight away feel like you had entered a joyous feast. Everyone would be chatty and having fun. People with a kitchen here like to have big meals, and enjoy the whole eating experience.

Just like any boisterous family, those with a kitchen here are prone to fights. But, who cares? They're family, and all is always forgiven. Most importantly, they love spending time and being playful together in the house. Anyone cooking in this area will cook a lot, and there's always plenty to go around. But, although they buy a lot of food, they'll only eat a little. They just love buying food for other people and making every meal a feast. On the other hand, if someone with a kitchen in this area lives alone, they'd probably hardly ever use the kitchen. Unless of course, they had guests.

Most people, whose kitchen is in this area, never eat just one kind of food. They love to try different things, and there will be a variety of dishes to choose from whenever they cook. Each big and full of flavor. No matter how much they prepare, they usually won't keep leftovers. They'd rather eat something new each day.

And nobody will really worry about how the food looks, as long as it tastes good. Don't worry about formalities here either as all they care about is enjoying each other's company.

#1. KEY FAMILY DYNAMICS
- Very close family
- Loud and fun
- Spend lots of time together
- Argue often but never lasting

#1. KEY DINING HABITS
- Eat big meals
- Love variety
- Not worried about presentation
- Cook a lot

#2. Kitchen In Adult 3rd-Sex Area

3	🮲🮳	1
4	9	8
5	6	7

Everyone in this house has their own routines. They won't all eat together at the same time. In their lives, every day is different. Even if someone cooks for everyone, the others will just grab a plate when they want it.

On rare occasions in which they do sit together, they won't talk much. Any conversation at the dinner table in this area will be small talk, never serious or personal. A family with the kitchen in the adult 3rd-sex area likes to keep things pleasant, but don't feel the need to share their private lives with each other. Especially family.

A kitchen in this area will only be used when the owner feels like it. They aren't the type for regular meal times or dining habits. Instead, they'll just cook whatever they're in the mood for in the moment. That's why, if someone here cooks from a recipe, they won't follow it word for word. They'll always do things in their own way.

Those with a kitchen here like to make everything look good when they cook. The problem is, if it looks good, it won't taste good. On the other hand, if it doesn't look good, it'll taste good. Basically, things in this area never happen how others expect them to turn out. Same with their relationships; when people living here think things are alright between them and others in the house, they usually aren't.

#2. Key Family Dynamics

- Everyone has their own lives.
- Don't spend much time together in the house.
- Pleasant but individually private.

#2. Key Dining Habits

- Never eat in routine.
- Only cook when in the mood.
- If the food looks good, it won't taste good and vice versa.
- Never follow recipes.

#3. Kitchen In Woman Area

[table]	2	1
4	9	8
5	6	7

This family loves routine. They come together every night at the same time, and all eat together. They like to make rules about how everything should be done. Usually, parents eating in this area will be disciplined with their children. They'll expect them to act politely, even when it's only the family eating together. Good manners and keeping up with appearances is important to this family.

If the dining area is in the Woman area, dining will be formal. Everything will be nicely set each time before they eat. Those living here also have routines for the kind of meals they eat each week. They have a reason for everything they eat too. For example, they may have meatloaf every Monday. Or they will make sure to eat carrots with every meal because they're good for your eyes.

In contrast to the adult 3rd-sex, when people cook a recipe in this area, they'll carefully follow each step of the recipe with precise measurement. They aren't the kind of people who can just throw something together. It has to be done in an orderly fashion.

#3. Key Family Dynamics

- Formal and disciplined.
- Have to look good in front of each other.
- Politeness and manners are important.

#3. Key Dining Habits

- Have meal routines.
- Eat everything for a reason.
- Formal table settings.
- Good manners expected from all diners.
- Food and presentation have to look good.

#4. Kitchen In Teenage Girl Area

3	2	1
🍽️	9	8
5	6	7

A teenage girl likes to keep to herself when she's at home. The people with a kitchen in this area are similar in this sense. When they're out and about, they'll like being social and around others. But once they're home, they want to have their own space.

A family with their kitchen in this area do care about each other but have a hard time expressing their feelings. So, they usually avoid talking about anything overly personal.

This kitchen will be used every day. Maybe not for a big meal, or at the same time each day. But you can be confident that someone will use it. Those living here love to stick to the food they know. They like to know what to expect. They're not the kind of people who like trying new things, foodwise. Individuals with a kitchen here will buy sweets regularly, but won't eat them often.

Those with a kitchen here won't like to have people over for dinner. They'd rather keep it private between family when at home. This family won't be talkative either. Except for occasionally talking about themselves.

#4. Key Family Dynamics

- Each person keeps to themselves.
- Avoid talking about personal issues.
- Like to keep family life and social life separate.

#4. Key Dining Habits

- Used every day.
- Eat the same food all the time.
- Don't like to have guests over for meals.

#5. Kitchen In Girl Area

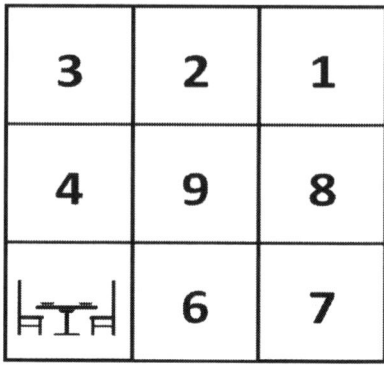

Just because people don't talk to each other all the time, doesn't mean they aren't close. It just means they don't feel the need to speak unless there is something they specifically want. This is how this family thinks. Those who cook and eat in this area of the house each has their own lives, and like it that way.

As you can imagine, little girls aren't the cooking type. They like it when other people to cook for them. Similarly, this kitchen won't often be used either. The inhabitants of this house probably stick to just making coffee, or at most, a sandwich or salad. They only like preparing things that are easy to cook. They'd rather go out to dinner anyway. Or bring something home.

#5. Key Family Dynamics

- Everyone has their own lives.
- Are close emotionally.
- Loose family relationships

#5. Key Dining Habits

- Never use the kitchen for cooking meals.
- Rather go out for meals.
- Only use the kitchen for little things like coffee.
- Usually, don't finish everything on their plate.

Quick Tip For Any Kitchen!

Make sure that open water isn't kept too close to the fire with which you cook. Otherwise, the water will evaporate and cool the surface temperature of food being prepared, which can cause health problems. Water vapors pick up germs and bacteria, which causes disease to spread quickly. Keep your kitchen clean and dry.

#6. Kitchen In Young 3rd-Sex Zone

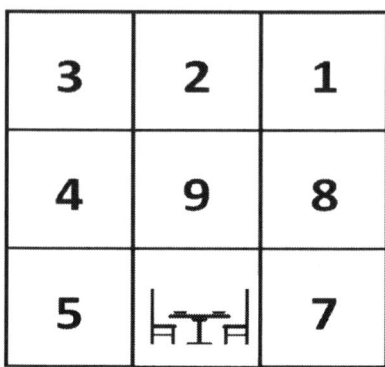

When a kitchen is in the 3-rd Sex Child area, chances are the only time people talk to each other, is when they're arguing. Similarly to the other "Child" areas at the front of a property, everyone in a house with a kitchen in this area will have separate lives and schedules. They won't spend time together while at home.

There's not much to say about cooking in this area. People here only eat to live, not for pleasure. The kitchen is simply not used for preparing food. The only thing they'd do is heat things up in the microwave or make coffee and tea. They'd never have a big family meal or break out the good cutlery for a formal dinner.

#6. Key Family Dynamic

- Only talk when arguing
- Not close when at home

- Don't spend time together

#7. Key Dining Habits

- Hardly cook at home, if ever
- Eats for nourishment, not for pleasure

#7. Kitchen In Young Boy Area

3	2	1
4	9	8
5	6	🪑🍽️🪑

This family is fun, talkative, and friendly. They're the kind of people who love sharing stories with one another. Luckily, they don't get into many fights, but when they do, they can get serious.

As far as cooking goes, anything prepared here will either look good and lack flavor, or will look unappetizing, but taste great. So, if you're given a dish that looks beautifully displayed, don't get your hopes up. Similar to the adult 3rd-sex zone. Except at least this one will still be tolerable when it's bad. People with a kitchen in this area generally enjoy bland food. They'll be fast eaters too.

Anyone cooking here will want to try new things, but won't ever stick to the recipe. They'll look up the ingredients to make something and buy what they need but never get around to actually making whatever it is. Like a little boy can be, people with a kitchen in the Young Boy Area can be quite clumsy. Expect regular accidents in this kitchen, like broken glasses or plates.

#7. KEY FAMILY DYNAMICS

- Talkative and friendly.
- Playful.
- Love to talk about themselves.
- Don't fight often. When do, it's big.

#7. KEY DINING HABITS

- Food either looks good and lacks flavor. Or looks unappealing but tastes great.
- Always loves to try new things
- Never sticks to recipes
- Usually, eat bland food
- In and out. Fast eaters.
- The most likely area to put ketchup on everything and to like fried foods.

#8. Kitchen In Teenage Boy Area

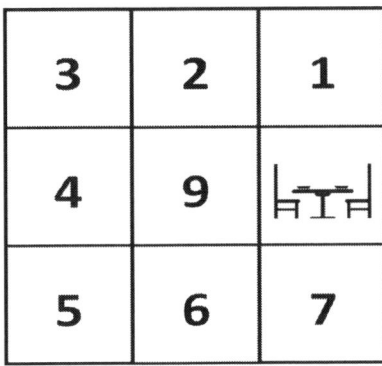

Teenage boys love lively get-togethers. It's a time for simple fun, food, and companionship. When everyone comes together for a meal in the Teenage Boy Area, they'll be talkative and choose to eat together for the social side of things. They don't care much about what they actually have for dinner.

Teenage boys like to try new things and can eat just about anything. They've got huge appetites. The same goes for people living here. So, if you're bringing something over, don't worry. They'll eat whatever you bring to the table. The more, the better.

A kitchen in this area reveals that the people living there like to invite others for dinner. They love it when people sit with them for a meal or chat. Dinner time is casual in this house. They're the "grab whatever you like" type of people and just enjoy being together. They can talk about anything too. They're so straightforward that onlookers may see them as sometimes speaking too bluntly. But that's just their way of being comfortable with others.

#8. Key Family Dynamics

- Love being together and socializing.
- Straightforward & often blunt.
- Open with each other.

#8. Key Dining Habits

- Casual diners.
- Eat a lot.
- Always try new things.
- Try things others wouldn't.
- Happy for others to join them.

#9. Kitchen In Family Area

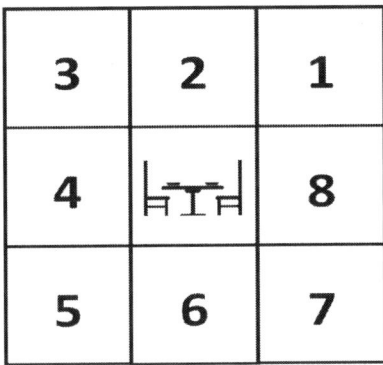

Finally, the family area. People living in a house with their kitchen in this area love spending time together. It's rare for anyone to ever be home alone. Just like any family, there will be frequent arguments between everyone, but nothing that can't be resolved.

A kitchen in this area is only used when they have people over, or if the whole family gets together for a meal. Nothing is ever done alone. If one person is cooking, others will jump in and help or at least do the dishes.

Eating here is a group activity. They care mostly about spending time together. But, even when they have a lot of people around them, these people will still often end up feeling lonely.

#9. Key Family Dynamics

- Love spending time together.
- Lots of little arguments.

- Rare to be alone.
- Feel lonely even when others are with them.

#9. Key Dining Habits

- Only cook when eating in a group.
- Never eat alone.
- Everyone helps each other in this kitchen.
- Always eat something different.

How To Pick A Great Restaurant Using Feng Shui

Each area of influence is ideal for a different style of cuisine. A kitchen in one area is excellent for Chinese food but terrible for traditional French cuisine. Each area of influence has its own strengths and weaknesses. When the area's character aligns with the cooking style used in a cuisine, the outcome is a great meal. But, when you cook the wrong style of food for the positioning of the kitchen, you'll end up with mediocre results, or worse.

These days people like to spend a lot of time eating out. And, most of us love trying new restaurants. But, they're often disappointing. No wonder we rely so much on reviews these days.

But, what if you could know how food would taste in any restaurant, before even sitting down? It's possible. You just need to know where the kitchen is.

We've listed a few favorite cuisines and the best area in which to prepare them. From now on, whenever you go out to dinner, you'll know how to pick the best food in town, anywhere in the world.

LOCAL TRADITIONAL FOOD

Who's the best at routine? Anything that doesn't have to change often, and needs to be cooked the same way, ever time, is best prepared in a kitchen within the Teenage Girl Area.

FUSION (FRENCH/ASIAN, AMERICAN/INDIAN)

No-one blends different styles together like the 3rd-Sex. If you're looking to enjoy fusion or a creative style of cuisine, look for a restaurant with a kitchen in the Adult 3rd-Sex Area. You'll enjoy tasty and unique dishes you never thought of before.

GOURMET & FINE DINING

Thinking about going somewhere special for a seven-course meal with full silver service using an array of cutlery? If you're looking for fine dining or something that takes precision, nothing beats a restaurant with a kitchen in the Woman's Area. The level of detail in preparation and presentation will be immaculate.

Chinese Food/ Indian Food

Any food where you eat large dishes shared by many, such as Chinese or Indian cuisines, is best prepared in the Man's Area. They won't use measuring cups or care much about how it looks. But it'll end up being a delicious feast.

Buffet

Just like Chinese or Indian food, buffets are big dining experiences. When going to a buffet, you want a variety of great-tasting fresh dishes in ample portions. This is again the Man Area's specialty. It's great for anything big, that's slightly chaotic, with lots of dishes.

Sandwich/Noodles/ Snacks

Sometimes we want something quick and easy. If you're looking for great tasting quick meals, like a sandwich, wrap or bowl of noodles, it's best to pick a place where they prepare it in the Young Boy Area. By the way, ever notice where Subway usually puts their sandwich preparation benches? Yep. That's right. In the Young Boy Area.

Desserts

We all like to have comfort food now and then. Ice cream, chocolate, pastries and other desserts are all best prepared in the Young Girl Area. Remember, it's the area for emotional choices.

ANYTHING THAT'S NOT TOO SPECIAL

The Teenage Boy Area is suitable for any kind of food, as long as it doesn't require any special skills for preparation. Easy meals will be tasty in a restaurant with a kitchen here.

Cooking Practice 3: *Fred's Kitchen*

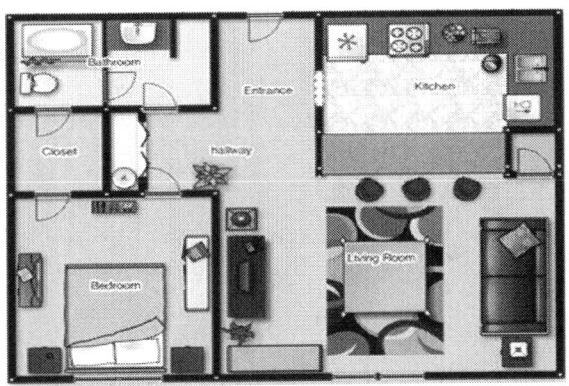

We know that Fred loves to be out of the house often. That he spends his money on routine and little things. Plus that he keeps his house tidy and presentable. But what can we tell from his kitchen? Is he a master chef at home? Or, does he have his favorite pizza place on speed dial?

His kitchen is in the back right, which is the man area. Usually, if the kitchen is in this area, it means that the person living there likes to cook in big amounts. But because Fred lives by himself, it shows that he wouldn't use this kitchen that often. He'd only use it if he had guests over. Then, Fred would probably host a lively feast.

Quick Quiz

QUESTION 1.

If the kitchen is in the Teenage Boy Area, what best describes the person's cooking/eating style?

- A. Formal and at the same time every day.
- B. Casual, big appetites and like to eat anything.
- C. Don't use the kitchen. Only for coffees, etc.

QUESTION 2.

When a bedroom is in the Adult 3rd-Sex area, the person sleeping there is best described as:

- A. A deep sleeper, decisive, loves new things and single focused.
- B. Romantic, organized, punctual, plans ahead.
- C. Creative, everything depends on mood, thinks different.

QUESTION 3.

Which toilet direction reveals that the person likely spends all their money each month?

A. Perpendicular to the road.
B. Parallel to the road.

Question 4.

What best describes the key characteristics of the Young Girl Area?

A. Emotional, bossy, active imagination, attention-seeking.
B. Underappreciated, thinks differently, only good at routine.
C. Casual, show off, straightforward, loves a challenge.

CHAPTER 10
The Living Room

Friends & Social Life

THE LIVING ROOM is where our private life connects to our social environment. It's usually the main room we use when having visitors over. The living room is mostly used to entertain and enjoy the company of, friends. That' why the living room reveals a lot about a person's social life and how they think about their friends.

By looking at this area of a house, we can see how people act with their friends while in the house, as well as how often they entertain guests. We also see whether they use the room frequently or not. Now, let's connect the living room with the areas of influence.

#1. Living Room In Man Area

3	2	🛋️
4	9	8
5	6	7

Imagine a typical man. Do you think he likes to have friends over? Or, would he keep his home private? If he did have visitors, how would they act when together? Would they be quiet, reserved, and well-mannered? Probably not. When the average man has friends over, they like to talk and laugh. Above all else, they just care about having a fun and relaxing time. Guys don't care about appearances. They just want a space where they can be themselves and enjoy the moment.

A living room is this area reveals that the people living here love to entertain guests, although they wouldn't have friends over all the time. When they have visitors in this area, it's high-energy with lots of talking. On the other hand, when family members sit here, they don't speak much. Only when it's necessary.

For this household, comfort is the number one priority. These people don't worry about how everything looks, as long as it's comfortable. They're likely to have big comfy couches and armchairs. The kind of furniture made to spend extended periods of time on. A living room in this position is for relaxation.

When people use this room, you know they're planning on being there a while. Maybe they like to watch movies, read, or just relaxing. Whatever it is, once they're there, they're there for a while.

People living here also like to show off to their friends. They're likely to spend money on things like big TVs, surround sound systems, and luscious couches. And they're more than happy to show others their prized possessions or seize an opportunity to talk about them.

#1. KEY SOCIAL CHARACTERISTICS

- Love to entertain.
- Love talking with others but only speaks when necessary with family.
- Big, lively get-togethers.
- Love spending time in large groups.
- Like to show off to friends.
- Easy to get annoyed with others.

#1. KEY ROOM HABITS

- Love to lounge for extended periods of time.
- Comfort is king.
- Spend money on good couches, TVs, and living room furniture.

#2 Living Room In Adult 3rd-Sex Area

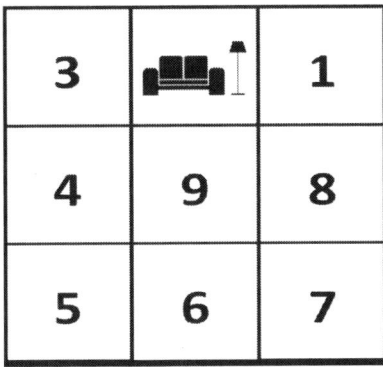

A living room in this area reveals that those living here aren't the kind of people who like to entertain guests often. When they do have visitors, they won't speak much other than small talk, while in this room. Unless, of course, they have specific shared interests.

This is consistent with the Adult 3rd-Sex personality. They're great in social settings, but would rather keep their private lives, private. They won't share many in-depth details about themselves. For example, it would be almost impossible for anyone to start any "deep-and-meaningful" personal conversations in this room.

Those living here want to look perfect in their friends' eyes. No matter how many problems they have in their lives, they'll never talk about them with friends. They're afraid they might look bad.

If multiple people, or a family, live here who all like to use the room, for example, to watch movies or TV, they'll sit together quietly, without interacting with each other. They aren't the kind of people who chat through a movie. When in this living room, you'll also notice that everything which looks comfortable, won't be. But that's ok, you won't want to spend much time there anyway.

#2. KEY SOCIAL CHARACTERISTICS

- Don't entertain often.
- Only engage in small talk with guests.
- Sit together but don't interact with each other.
- Only talk with each other if they've got similar interests and personalities.

#2. KEY ROOM HABITS

- Won't spend much time in this room.
- Don't use it routinely, depends on mood.

#3. Living Room In Woman Area

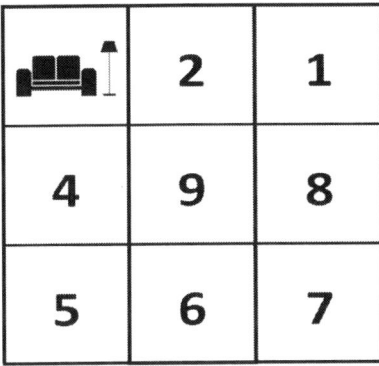

Keeping up appearances is important for many people. Especially those with a living room in the Woman's Area of influence. Actually, maybe we shouldn't call it a living room. Because if it's in this area, it's more of a showcase for visitors.

Those living here have formal living rooms, with everything in its special place. Great care is taken to decorate the area, and you can be sure this room is kept neat and tidy at all times. Just in case someone important comes by.

In a woman's mind, it's essential to maintain a good image of themselves. They feel it's importance to be well-presented in any social setting. For example, many women will put on makeup to go to the supermarket, just in case they bump into someone they know. Whereas a man can go out to dinner with friends in dirty jeans and simply forget to shave for a week.

People with a living room in the Woman's Area only invite those into their homes who they feel are important. They want visitors they can impress with their kind hospitality and attractive setting. Conversations in this area are usually pleasant and well-mannered but straight forward. But it's as if they're wearing a social mask.

#3. KEY SOCIAL CHARACTERISTICS

- Formal social life.
- Social life used for keeping up appearances.
- Likes to spend time in small groups or one on one.
- Have to look good in public.

#3. KEY ROOM HABITS

- Use the room often and routinely
- Everything kept tidy.
- Decorative.

#4. Living Room In Teenage Girl Area

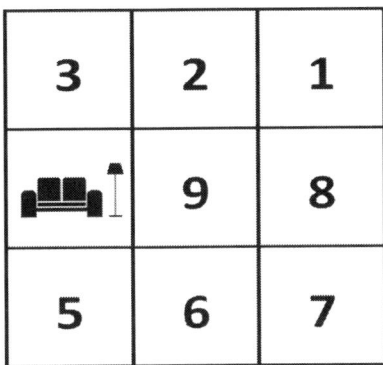

Nearly every Hollywood teen movie shows how "clicky" teenage girls can be. In a typical flick, there are always small cluster groups of friends, who have something in common, and the shared perception of others being strange or different. Normally, teenage girls will have a set group of friends who they share everything in their lives with. But, they're hesitant to accept new people into their group. They'd rather keep their social circles small.

Individuals who have a living room in the Teenage Girl Area tend to be the same. They'll only invite certain people, who they trust, into their homes. If they have guests over, it'll be in small groups.

Those living here prefer to go out to socialize. These people feel that their home is a private space. On the occasions that they do have people over, they'll always first clean up a little. They'll feel that their living room is usually too messy for hosting guests. When sitting here with friends, they'll be straight forward and often have strong opinions to share during conversations.

#4. Key Social Characteristics

- Have a small circle of close friends.
- Like to go out to socialize.
- Keep home & social life separate.
- Want to look good for their friends & guests.
- Speak straight forward.
- Highly Opinionated.

#4. Key Room Habits

- Room will be messy.
- Will tidy up for guests.
- Won't use the room often.

#5. Living Room In Young Girl Area

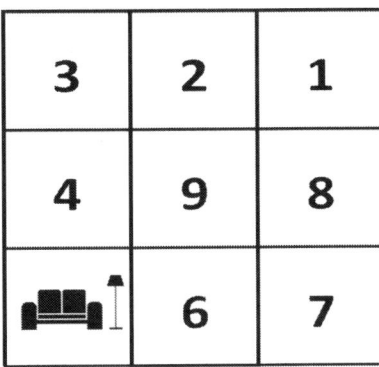

How are young girls in social settings? It depends whether they know the people they're talking to or not. For most, the picture of a shy, young girl, hiding behind her mother's dress when meeting new people, is a familiar one.

No matter how outspoken or confident young girls are with their family members, they're naturally reserved around new people. They'll often cling to their mother or father, or be reserved around people they aren't used to. Young girls usually have a hard time trusting people outside their family. They're wary, and spend a lot of time watching people before engaging with them.

Those with a living room in this area won't typically allow visitors into their homes. They want to keep their home private, only allowing only those they've known for a long time in. On the rare occasion that they do have people over, they're likely to ask lots of questions out of curiosity. But, won't remember people's answers.

#5. Key Social Characteristics

- Don't like to mingle with new people.
- Slow to warm up to new people.
- Only invite trusted friends over.
- Love their social comfort zone.

#5. Key Room Habits

- Won't use the room often.
- When speaking to someone there, they'll ask many questions but won't remember much.

#6. Living Room In Young 3rd-Sex Area

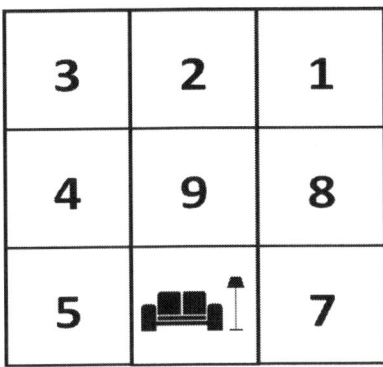

The young 3rd-sex is a private individual. They're deeply involved within their own minds and feel different than their peers. 3-rd Sex children rather being by themselves than in a group. In general, they don't often want to socialize with others. When they do, they more content to listen and aren't generally talkative. They'll usually only speak when someone asks them a question. People whose living room is in this area will share the same social traits. They don't care much about maintaining an active social life when at home. They'll be good listeners when with their friends and rather hear about other's lives than sharing things about their own.

If a family lives in this house, the room would generally be used by only one person at a time. If multiple people happened to be in the room, it's likely that they wouldn't talk to each other at all. They'd each do their own thing.

#6. KEY SOCIAL CHARACTERISTICS

- Private people.
- Like being by themselves.
- Good listeners.
- Only speak when people ask them questions.

#6. Key Room Habits

- Hardly ever uses the room.
- Don't use it for social occasions.
- Normally only one person at a time.

#7. Living Room In Young Boy Area

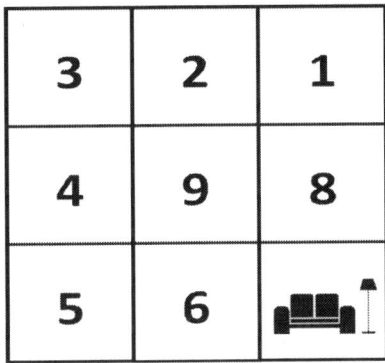

When watching a young boy play with others, you'll quickly notice how seemingly impossible it is for him to sit still for any extended period of time. They love to be active. Exploring the world and playing with their newest toys. They're always coming up with new and exciting things to do. Likewise, people with a living room in the Young Boy Area live active social lives, but not in the house.

They might watch a movie, or sit and chat on the phone, but you'll never find them lazing about or relaxing there for extended periods of time. If they have friends over, they won't be in the living room long either. They'll generally just stop by or sit there waiting to go out somewhere. If the visitors are staying for a while, they'll do it in a different area of the house.

Just like a young boy, these people love anything new. For example, they won't watch the same movie twice. They'll always want fresh experiences when in that room.

#7. Key Social Characteristics

- Love meeting new people.
- Always keep active.
- Playful and fun with friends.

#7. Key Room Habits

- If friends come over, it's not for long.
- When in the room they'll talk a lot, but only a small amount will be useful.
- Don't sit still for long.
- Never watch the same thing twice

#8. Living Room In Teenage Boy Area

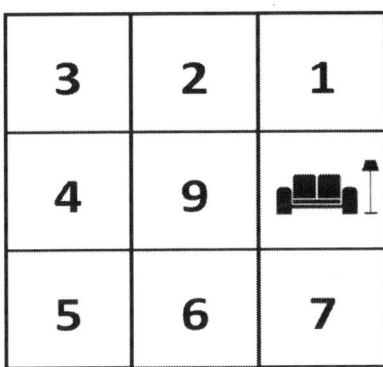

Imagine a teenage boy spending time with friends. How would you describe the scene? Would it in a big group or small? How does he interact with his buddies? Is he well mannered? You'd mostly likely assume that teenage boys are highly social. It's true. Teenage boys love spending time doing anything they can with their friends. They aren't picky. They just want to have fun.

Those with a living room in the Teenage Boy Area will share similar social traits. For them, the living room is a place of comfort. A teenage boy knows the real meaning of relaxation. If you visit a home with the living room in this area, don't worry about being polite, quiet or even tidy. These people love chitchatting about anything, except themselves.

But, just like any male teenager, don't expect them to do anything for you either. For them, it's "my house, is your house." If you want a drink, they'll point you in the direction of the fridge and tell you to grab it yourself.

#8. Key Social Characteristics

- Highly social.
- Casual hosts, each to their own.
- Large groups and talkative.
- Likes to talk about anything other than themselves.

#8. Key Room Habits

- Completely relaxed when here.
- Not tidy.
- Will use the room often.
- Love having visitors here.

#9. Living Room In Family Area

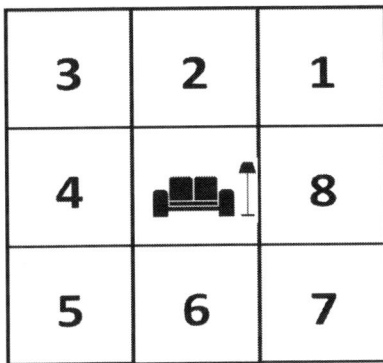

In a big family, there is rarely a moment when people aren't interacting with others. There's always some kind of gathering happening, whether just with members of the family, or visitors coming by to see someone in the house. In the same way, those with a living room in the Family Area won't generally sit in the room by themselves.

If they're at home alone, they'll spend most their time in other areas of the house. This leads back to the idea that a family simply isn't a family if there's only one person. That's why if someone lives by themselves in this house, they'll only use the room when they have others over for a social gathering.

People with a living room in the Family Area will have visitors frequently and are able to chat with people from all walks of life. This is a great room for sitting down for a chat.

#9. Social Habits

- Constantly with other people. Hardly ever alone
- Often have gatherings
- Can talk to people from all walks of life

#9. Room Habits

- Only use when groups, never alone.
- Good place for chatting

Living Practice 4.
Fred's Living Room

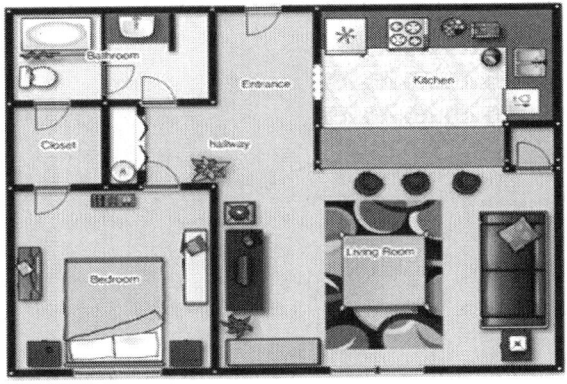

As you've just learned, the living room represents a person's social life. When we look at the area it's in, we can see how the inhabitant of a house spends their time with friends. What area of influence is Fred's living room in? It's at the front of his apartment, on the right-hand side. This is the Young Boy Area. What can we tell about Fred's life from this?

Firstly, we know that he doesn't spend much time in the room. It's likely that Fred has an active social life but doesn't bring his friends back to his house. If they do happen to come by, they'll be just stopping by for a short period of time.

CHAPTER 11
The Office
Work Style

MANY PEOPLE have an area in their home dedicated to their work. They may run a business from their home office, catch up on work outside of business hours, or use the space for managing the household's finances. Just like any of the other room in a house, the area of influence in which the office is located will affect their behavior. In this case, their work.

The home office's location reveals a person's work style and how much time they spend there. This is also true for any commercial workspace areas. This chapter will give you an idea of how your desk's location within an office building influences your work style. Plus by the end, we share some Feng Shui tips for greater productivity. Let's start with the areas and their impact on work.

#1. Office In Man Area

3	2	🖥️
4	9	8
5	6	7

If we describe a typical male's work style, what assumptions could we make? We wouldn't guess him to be skilled at multitasking first of all. But, he could excel at highly specialized tasks which require single-minded concentration. When a man does anything he considers to be his duty, he's able to maintain high levels of concentration for extended periods of time. Think of the guards at Buckingham Palace. You'd never see a young girl or boy with that determination to stay in one spot for so long. But, men aren't generally good at delegation. They usually try to do everything themselves.

Let's translate this into work habits we'd see in someone with an office or home workspace in the man area. When they're at their desks, we can assume that they'll be there for extended periods of time. They wouldn't be routine-driven and or schedule their time the same way each day. Because, when they work, they become so involved with it all that they lose track of time. They'd also make little mistakes with detail oriented tasks. The good thing about people working in the Man Area is that they're skilled at big-picture thinking. They're good at setting and achieving lofty goals and targets for themselves.

This area used to be ideal for quick decision making. Now, technology has created a flood of constantly changing information. The world is moving quickly, and new data is available every minute of the day. This has made the male character more contemplative before making important decisions. They're a little more doubtful of their choices because they don't know how things may change in the future.

#1. KEY WORK CHARACTERISTICS

- Good at big-picture thinking.
- Makes mistakes in the details.
- Stubborn and want things done their way.
- Single-minded.
- Confident/Stubborn in what they do.
- Contemplative but decisive.

#1. KEY ROOM HABITS

- Spends extended periods of time there.
- Is likely to frequently lose track of time.

SPECIAL RETAIL SHOP MENTION

If a store's sales counter is in the Man Area, it means that they will wait to collect big amounts of money before moving it elsewhere. This store is likely to get big ticket sales, but not frequently.

#2 Office In Adult 3rd-Sex Area

3		1
4	9	8
5	6	7

The adult 3rd-sex is a creative individual. They're "out of the box" thinkers and know how to think differently than anyone else. They always find their own way of getting things done.

People working here will be similar to a duck. A duck can do many things (swim, walk, fly) but is a master of none. Those working in the Adult Third Sex Area are similar. They're good at many things, but not highly skilled in any one thing.

An office in this area reveals the person working there to be creative in their work process. They love coming up with new ideas and trying new ways to get things done. This is a great space for brainstorming fresh ideas.

Those working in the Adult Third Sex Area love to receive recognition for their work. A little praise will go a long way with people working in this location. But, critics be warned. If they're told something bad about their work, it'll fall on deaf ears. They feel like whatever they create is marvelous.

This area isn't good for those doing routine work or for people needing to make decisions quickly. Whoever works here gets bored quickly and always does things their way.

#2. Key Work Habits

- Always come up with their own way to do things.
- Good with creative work.
- Get bored easily with routine work.
- Are able to do many different things but aren't the best at any of them.
- Have difficulty making decisions.
- Stubborn and never feel their work is wrong.

#2. Key Room Habits

- People working in this space will not be here for a predictable period of time. It will change every day according to their moods.

Special Retail Shop Mention

This is not a good area for sales or inventory maintenance. If a retail store's sales counter is in this area, they'll wait until the last moment before making a decision to re-order stock.

#3. Office In Woman Area

🖥️	2	1
4	9	8
5	6	7

Woman do things differently than men. On average, women are naturally adept at detail-orientated tasks. They notice things a man misses. Ask any married woman. Women are usually more organized than men and care about things looking right.

Likewise, someone working in the Woman's Area is detailed in everything they do. They double or triple-check their work, worrying about the all the specifics. They'll be good at delegating, and overseeing another's performances. People who work in this area of the house or office like structure in their activities. They sit down to work at the same time each day, keep everything in its place, and maintain set procedures to get things done. They're the kind of people who work with checklists and agendas.

The bad thing about this area is that it isn't good for flexibility. It is difficult for those here to come up with fresh ideas. If a creative designer sat here, they would be too concerned with details which would stifle their creativity and lead to poor results.

People here like to plan to the tiniest details, but nothing ever seems to go to plan. If they plan on something, it won't happen. But if they don't plan for it, it will.

#3. Key Work Habits

- Like to plan their days ahead of time
- Everything structured and step-by-step
- Things go opposite to plan
- Think a lot.
- Bad at creative tasks
- Good delegators. Are able to enlist others' help.
- Good with details

#3. Key Room Habits

- Frequent and routine use.
- Well-organized and tidy
- Keeps things looking beautiful.

Special Mention

Those working here tend to be frugal and think a lot before spending money. They like to buy things for their business that builds their image or look.

#4. Office In Teenage Girl Area

3	2	1
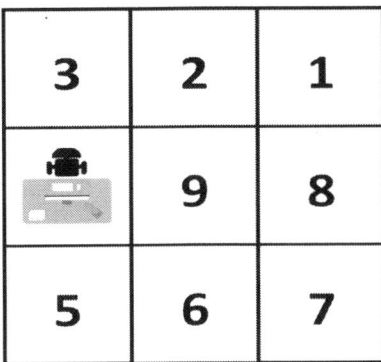	9	8
5	6	7

Most teenage girls are more studious than teenage boys. They show more interest in academics, learning, and whatever they consider their responsibility. You're more likely to find a teenage girl sitting in her room, happily reading a book than a teenage boy.

Similarly, those with their workspace in this area of a house or office will be good at routine duties. As long as they have structure and direction, they'll be okay. They can especially excel at anything to do with paperwork, regular administrative duties, or financial management tasks such as bookkeeping or accounting. They also spend a lot of time on research things before deciding anything. On the other hand, this also means that they're slow decision makers. Because they don't like being wrong.

They are the kind of people who prefer doing things by themselves. They'd rather get things done without having to rely on, or talk to, others. They also don't like to get involved with other people's business when it comes to working. If it isn't their duty, they won't bother with it.

#4. KEY WORK CHARACTERISTICS

- Good with routine work.
- Great when given specific tasks to do.
- Not good at thinking for themselves what to do.
- Must be told their specific duties.
- Rather work alone than in a team setting.
- Slow decision makers.
- Spend time collecting much information before making decisions.

#4. KEY ROOM HABITS

- Like to work in privacy.
- Workspace isn't tidy, but they know where everything is.

SPECIAL MENTION

This is a good place to put people who work with large quantities of data. They'll be detailed with paperwork related tasks, such as quality control, and insurance or legal contracts.

#5. Office In Young Girl Area

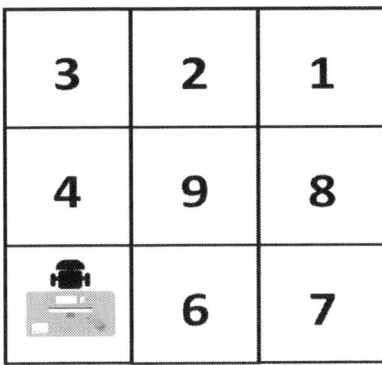

It may be hard to imagine a young girl working hard behind a desk. But consider how a young girl acts when she feels that something is important or her duty. Just try to tell a young girl that it doesn't matter where her Barbie sleeps in the dollhouse. She'll think that you lost your mind or simply don't know what you're talking about. Whatever she thinks is important, is, in her mind. Not only does it matter but she feels that others should see the importance of everything she does too.

Those working in this area will have certain similarities. They'll think that their job is important, and feel that they deserve recognition for their work. When they do anything, they want it to look good. But, the actual quality of work will depend largely on their emotions at the time. People working in the Young Girl Area are generally good delegators but come across as bossy. Not that they care, though. They'll also love being talkative at work, but only to talk about anything other than their job.

#5. Key Work Characteristics

- Talkative while working.
- Bossy.
- Craves recognition and acknowledgment of how important they are.
- Results depend on their mood at the time.
- Skilled at making things look good.

#5. Key Room Habits

- Won't spend much time in this room.
- If they stay here for longer periods of time, they'll be communicating with others on the phone or computer.
- Room or office space will often be messy.

Special Mention

This is a good place for customer service or support staff to sit. They'll talk a lot, and ask many questions. They like being chatty.

#6. Office In Young 3rd-Sex Area

Being different from those around you can be challenging. The Young 3rd-Sex character doesn't like drawing attention to themselves in the workplace. They'd rather be in the background, doing their own thing. Being and thinking differently puts one in an awkward position where what they consider good, others will see as bad. It's impossible for those in the Young 3-rd Sex Area to hold leadership or creative positions. They prefer others to make decisions for them anyway. They're better in support roles where they can help others. However, they can become so busy helping others that their own work doesn't get finished.

Those working in the Young 3-rd Sex Area are happy to follow orders and good at routine tasks. But, if not kept busy, they won't take the initiative to come up with things to do. It's also difficult for them to maintain focus on their work because they're so involved with their own world.

#6. Key Work Characteristics

- Think differently than others in the office.
- Are often under-appreciated.
- Hard time making decisions.
- Great at routine or following orders.
- Not skilled at creative work or self-guiding.

#6. Key Room Habits

- Won't spend extended periods of time in this position.
- When here will be in their own world, either through using online devices or immersed in their work.

Special Mention

If a cash register is in this area, products will be sold for less than the price they should be. On the other hand, this is a good area for deep discount bins and anything which is seen to be of little to no value.

#7. Office In Young Boy Area

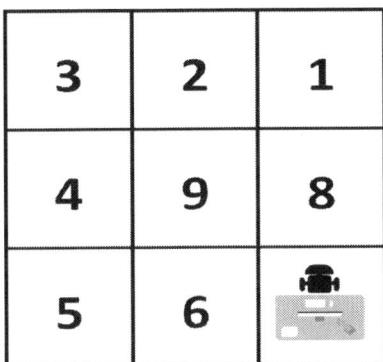

A young boy jumps right in whenever something needs to be done. But, 5 mins later they're off doing something completely different. Young boys have extremely short attention spans. If something isn't interesting, new, or exciting, they'll lose interest and just watch the clock, waiting to leave.

Similarly, those working in the young boy area have the same job mentality. They aren't the kind of people who can sit diligently at their desks for extended periods of time. Unless, of course, they're using the internet to mentally travel. Any detailed or routine work is considered too boring for these people. It's probably one of the worst areas for people to work in if their job involves routine or paperwork.

Those working here will excel at anything to do with new ideas, new technology, or pleasing others. For example, customer service centers or help desks. Beware, those working in the Young Boy Area have a tendency to start multiple projects without finishing them.

#7. Key Work Characteristics

- Does everything quickly, but makes mistakes.
- Quickly bored with routine.
- Good with anything fast-paced.
- Adaptable. Likes variety.
- Starts lots of projects but never finishes them.
- Excellent in customer service roles.

#7. Key Room Habits

- Won't spend much time here. They're restless.
- If they're here for an extended period of time, they will mentally be somewhere else. Such as on the phone or communicating with others online.

Special Mention

This area is ideal for any retail locations which have small amounts of money coming in and out all the time. For example, a 7-11. If the cash register is in this area, they'll do very well.

#8. Office In Teenage Boy Area

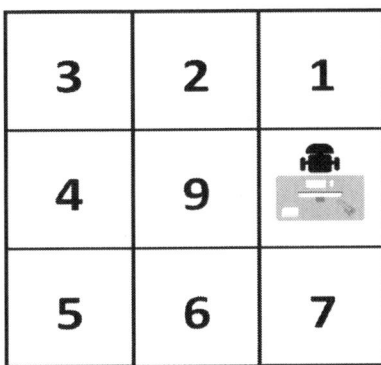

Hitting goals, achieving the highest score on their favorite game or performing daring stunts, are all things that teenage boys love to do. Put them in a position where they're able to prove their skills, while spending time with others, and they're happy. That's why this space works well for sales staff.

An office or workspace in this area reveals that the person working here enjoys challenging work, and like to interact with lots of people. In an office building, whoever sits here is most likely close to other staff members and chatty with their colleagues. Whoever works here is also good at anything that needs to stay up to date with current trends and technology.

Teenage boys don't like to sit when they working. They'd rather move around. If someone has to sit here for long periods of time, they'll likely be using the internet to at least mentally move about. A teenage boy is terrible with schedules or planning. Similarly, those working here won't spend a lot of time and effort making detailed plans. They're more focused on action. But be careful, if you give people working here a routine job or things to do with paperwork, it either won't get done at all or if it is done, it'll be done sloppily.

#8. Key Work Characteristics

- Good at competitive work.
- Love interacting with other people.
- Terrible at routine work.
- If given regular work they'll make frequent mistakes.
- Good with flexible work structures and tasks.
- Skilled at adapting to new things.
- Current and up to date with everything.

#8. Key Room Habits

- Will often talk with others around them.
- Won't be able to sit still for extended periods of time.

Special Mention

If a retail counter is here, most people who pay here will use credit cards rather than cash. This reflects the teenager's affiliation with technology.

#9. Office In Family Zone

Remember, there's always more than one person to a family. Likewise, there's nearly always more than one person in this area or no one at all. No matter what the room is used for. If this is a single office space, it'll likely remain empty and instead be used for storage or the like. But, if someone does work here, they'll have to regularly solve other people's problems.

The good thing is that a desk in this area shows the person to be great at multi-tasking and good at routine work. It's is also a good place for product distribution. Anything that allows for revenue to come in from many different angles. In an office building, this space is useful to conduct meetings.

#9. Key Work Characteristics

- Multi-tasking
- Fixing other people's problems

- Never working alone.

#9. KEY ROOM HABITS

- Only used when more than one person is there
- Often used for storage or many different things in one place.

SPECIAL MENTION

When handling money in this area of a property or structure, it means that there will be multiple revenue streams. The income cannot just come from one thing.

Office Tips

FILING SYSTEM

Unkept files or work kept directly behind where you sit when working, represents unfinished tasks. If you don't file things away carefully, you'll continuously have new work coming in before being able to finish previous responsibilities. By filing everything away properly, you'll be able to complete each task on time.

The 9 Areas of a Desk

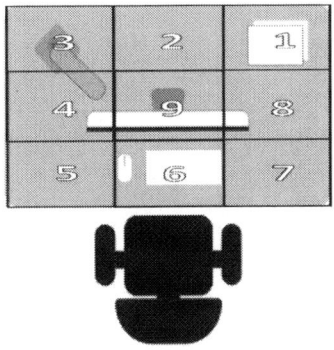

Just like the area of land or structure, a desk can also be broken down into the 9 distinct areas of influence. But instead of aligning the grid from the front road, it's done from where we face the desk. The area closest to the chair represents the child areas. The back right is the man area, the back left is the woman, and so on. The adult areas are regarded as having the highest importance. Similarly to the fact that we pay respects to our elders.

A problem arises if you leave your "In" tray or to-do pile in one of the desk's adult areas. If this is the case for your desk, you'll constantly have important tasks that need your immediate attention, and no matter what you're currently doing. This constant interruption makes it difficult to get any work done.

The front child areas are where the most movement occurs. Anything on your desk in these regions is interacted with regularly and will often come and go from your desk. For this reason, it's better to keep any work that needs to be done in the child areas, to help you complete tasks quickly and move on to the next.

When thinking about where to place your computer on a table, consider what you use the computer for. If you mostly use the computer for emails and communication, putting the computer in the Teenage Boy Area would be a good idea. But, if you need to make sure everything you do is perfect, then the #3 Woman Area would be better. Each area of the desk is good for something different. Look back at the characteristics and strengths of each area to pick which one is best for you.

The Desk's Direction

The direction a person faces when sitting at their desk reveals how aware they are of everything that happens in their business or office. Either they know what everyone else is doing in the business and everything going on. Or, they're only aware of their own responsibilities. Both have their own value depending on the person's actual job.

No direction is good or bad, per se. They can only be right or wrong for that particular set of circumstances. For example, if you are a columnist, there is no need to know what everyone else is doing in the company. But, if you are in management, it's in your best interest to be aware of what's happening throughout the company. That way you can prepare for the future and direct your staff accordingly.

Facing Towards The Road

When facing the road from their work chair, a person will know about everything happening in their work environment. They'll be aware of things to come and be able to plan ahead. This is useful if they need to know every detail of what's happening in the business.

When the person sitting here is already a detail-oriented individual, they'll become meticulous to the point where others may feel that they're micromanaging everything. Some staff won't be able to handle that. Likewise, if the person working here doesn't need to know what others are doing, they may become too involved in others' business, rather than focusing on their own tasks.

Facing Parallel To The Road

If someone sits at their desk with the road on their left or right as they work, they'll know some, but not all, things happening in their work environment.

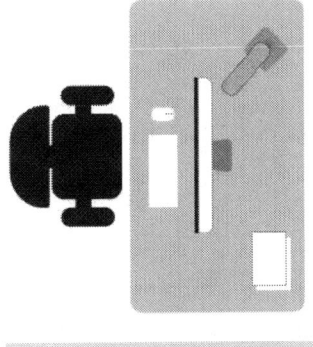

This is useful for people who need to be kept in the loop on some things, but don't need to know everything.

Facing Away From The Road

If you're in a job or position where you don't need to know everything going on around you and instead want to focus solely on your own work, it's best to face away from the road.

People facing away from the road won't have a clue about most things happening outside of their range of duties. It can be useful for routine or creative work. However, the problem is that they won't see problems or changes ahead of time, which will make it impossible for this person to plan anything.

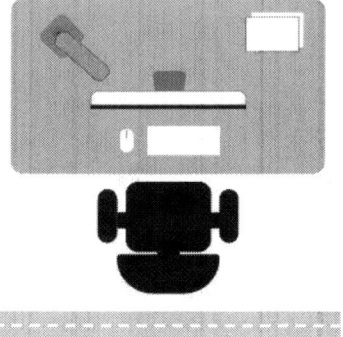

CHAPTER 12
Honorable Mentions

THERE ARE COMPONENTS to the average house, other than rooms, which we should discuss. In this chapter, we'll cover three or them. Firstly, we'll look at the importance of stairs when looking at a person's behavior at home. Then, how open bodies of water like swimming pools and water features impact the health and emotions of everyone in a house. Lastly, there's a special section on trees and what they reveal about the inhabitants of a house. Let's start.

The Staircase

A staircase reveals how people uses them, depending on the area of the structure. In a home, this provides us with a clearer picture of their habits at home (do they spend a lot of time upstairs vs. do they keep going up and down all the time).

Whereas, in some businesses, the staircase leads to a stock room. In which case, the staircase can mean a lot. Frequent visits up and down the stairs could indicate high sales as they would need to frequently retrieve stock for example.

#1. Stairs In Man Area

When anyone goes upstairs, they'll stay there for a long time. It's unlikely for them to go up and down frequently each day. Usually, they'll spend either all day downstairs or upstairs.

3	2	1
4	9	8
5	6	7

#2. Stairs In 3Rd-Sex Area

People here use the stairs often. But, they don't stay on any particular floor for long. They change their minds frequently. People living here generally can't stay in one place in the house for long.

3	2	1
4	9	8
5	6	7

#3. Stairs In Woman Area

Here, a staircase is also used quite often. People go up and down frequently. They'll move around a lot while at home. They'll constantly have things to do and regularly move from one room to another.

3	2	1
4	9	8
5	6	7

#4. Stairs In Teenage Girl Area

A staircase in the teenage girl area would hardly be used at all. They'd only go upstairs or down when it is really necessary.

3	2	1
4	9	8
5	6	7

#5. Stairs In Young Girl Area

These stairs wouldn't often be used, either. For example, people might only go upstairs to sleep at night. Guests generally wouldn't be invited upstairs unless they were close and trusted friends or family members.

3	2	1
4	9	8
5	6	7

#6. Stairs In Young 3Rd-Sex Area

People won't know whether someone is upstairs or downstairs. It seems like everyone in the house is in their own world. You know that feeling when you walked into a room and forgot what you were there for? This will frequently happen when going up or down these stairs.

3	2	1
4	9	8
5	6	7

#7. Stairs In Young Boy Area

They'll often be used. People will often be running up or down to get or do something.

3	2	1
4	9	8
5	6	7

#8. Stairs In Teenage Boy Area

They'll also use this staircase frequently. But when they do, people living here will usually move up or down quickly. Imagine a teenager jumping down three steps at a time. The problem with this house is that when you get downstairs, you'll realize that you forgot something upstairs. Then, once you are at the top of the stairs, you'll remember that you left something downstairs. This will happen all the time.

3	2	1
4	9	8
5	6	7

Swimming Pools & Water Features

Traditional Chinese Feng Shui often discusses the favorable "chi" or prosperity benefits derived from having water on a property. We'll share a different point of view.

Firstly, let's discuss the reason behind the common suggestion Feng Shui masters make of having a water feature in the house.

Many of years ago, we primarily grew our own foods, and collected water, for our survival. Wise advisors would usually suggest finding a piece of land with a natural source of water. Back then, more water meant more life and therefore more prosperity. So far so good. They also suggested having a hill at the back of the property. This protected young plants from destructive winds. The problem is that traditional Chinese Feng Shui hasn't been updated in centuries and is now out of sync with today's society.

We don't grow our own food anymore, nor do we need to collect our own water. Most people buy their food and have indoor plumbing to pump water.

The most significant open bodies of water we have on our properties are swimming pools and water features. These aren't naturally occurring. They're forced collections of water. The issue with this is – scientifically speaking – that they create breeding grounds for germs and disease. Microbes become airborne as the water naturally evaporates. Inhaling this concoction of bacteria and water particles then leads to immune system issues.

From a symbolic perspective, water is in a constant state of flux, and uncontrollable. Similar to our flow of emotions. When we combine the areas of influence with the meaning of the swimming pool, we see specifically who's emotions and health are mostly affected by the Feng Shui of the swimming pool.

#1. Swimming Pool In Man Area

The man of the house will be moody, and his emotions will change frequently. He'll have a difficult time keeping a stable mind. A

3	2	1
4	9	8
5	6	7

swimming pool here means that any man in the house is likely to be sick regularly.

When the land is replaced by the water, it cuts the man's area of influence. Therefore, all adult men in this house will behave similarly to teenage boys, rather than men.

#2. Swimming Pool In Adult 3Rd-Sex Area

The third sex Every represents every human, with both female and male characteristics. When a large body of water is in this area, both the men and the women in this house will have mood swings. There will also be many arguments in this house.

3	2	1
4	9	8
5	6	7

As for use, they would only swim in this pool when the mood arises. Those living here wouldn't routinely swim each morning or weekend as part of their exercise, for example.

#3. Swimming Pool In Woman Area

When the pool is in the Women's area of a property, it means that the adult women in the house will experience mood swings. They'll often fall ill as well, due to the location of the pool (or large water feature).

3	2	1
4	9	8
5	6	7

A swimming pool in this area of a house would often be used, but only for short periods of time. In this area, the pool is likely seen as a place for a quick dip, or daily exercise. They have specific reasons to get in the pool. Also, if the pool is here, people may be invited over for a pool party now and then, but they would mostly sit around as part of the setting, rather than jump in.

#4. Swimming Pool In Teenage Girl Area

Similarly to the woman's zone, a swimming pool in this area indicates that women in this house will have health issues. Especially so for any teenage girls living here.

3	2	1
4	9	8
5	6	7

The difference between the pool in this area and the Woman's Area is that the people here would never invite others to come over to spend time in or near the pool. Only those living in the house, and trusted close friends would be allowed to use it.

Lastly, a body of water in this area symbolizes a divide between the female adult and female child areas. This reveals that a mother and daughter living here would have communication problems, and often get into arguments with each other.

#5. Swimming Pool In Young Girl Area

If a couple living here want to have a child, it would be near impossible for them to have a girl.

3	2	1
4	9	8
5	6	7

Any young girl living in that house will suffer emotional ups and downs all the time. You'd probably see frequent temper tantrums here. Any young girls would also suffer from chronic health problems.

#6. Swimming Pool In Young 3Rd-Sex Area

Whenever there is a divide between two areas, communication issues or tensions arise. In this case, if a young girl and boy lived in this house, such as brother and sister, they wouldn't get along.

3	2	1
4	9	8
5	**6**	7

A swimming pool in this area wouldn't be used either. It would end up neglected and dirty.

#7. Swimming Pool In Young Boy Area

As you may guess by now, any young boys in this house will have emotional and health issues. Regarding use, this pool would be used purely for fun. You wouldn't find anyone using it to do laps or exercise. They'll only use it for short periods of pure enjoyment.

3	2	1
4	9	8
5	6	**7**

#8. Swimming Pool In Teenage Boy Area

This pool indicates a breakdown in communication between a father and their son, as it divides the adult and child areas associated with the two. If a family living here has a teenage boy, he'll frequently argue with his father. Accordingly, any teenage boy in this house will also suffer mood swings and regular sickness.

3	2	1
4	9	**8**
5	6	7

This pool would get a lot of use. These are the kind of people who are likely to have guests over for pool parties and a swim.

#9. Swimming Pool In Family Area

If the swimming pool in this area isn't kept immaculately clean, the whole family (or everyone in that house) will be moody and get into arguments with each other. Everyone living here is prone to recurring illness.

3	2	1
4	9	8
5	6	7

Perhaps more importantly, whatever good that comes into these people's lives can't last long. Their lives are unstable and fluctuating. Just like the water.

Trees

Trees are living sentient beings. Although not recognized by our current society as the same level as ourselves or animals, all plants have a sophisticated awareness and intellect. They sense their surroundings. They eat, breathe, and communicate to form relationships with others, just like animals or human beings. The extent of this is something that modern science is only now coming to realize.

Trees on a property are able to help people but can be harmful if used improperly. Trees hold together the earth beneath us, creating stability. They help absorb subtle vibrations caused by traffic and earth movements which subconsciously disturb our sleep. Trees literally support our life and home.

Trees also absorb excess heat and provide fresh air by exhaling oxygen and inhaling carbon dioxide during the daytime. However, every plant with leaves will release carbon dioxide during the evenings, which is why it's counterproductive to have leafy plants in any sleeping areas. The excess carbon dioxide creates long-term health issues for those sleeping with plants in their room.

Many past cultures had special relationships with trees. For some they represented fertility, to others, they embodied angels or guardian spirits. Either way, their significance has always been recognized by naturalistic cultures.

In Aur's style of Feng Shui, we know the intelligence and authentic sentient life a tree has. We're also able to see that the location of prominent trees on a property influences the inhabitants. This is done by connecting the concept that they contain a form of spirit or life-force symbolic to the character of that land with the 9 areas discussed in this book.

We won't cover all the areas of influence for trees. We'll outline the areas of a property where trees have the most noticeable impact on those living here. Namely the three adult areas, and the family area.

#1. Tree In Man Area

Each person in this house will be strong-willed and stubborn like a typical male. A tree in this area reveals that the man of the house will always have the support he needs in life. Trees here are likely to become massive.

3	2	1
4	9	8
5	6	7

#2. Tree In 3rd-Sex Adult Area

A tree in this area helps to balance both males and females in this house. It allows them to be stable and well-grounded. Having the kind of tree which has deep roots is good for this area. The deeper their roots, the calmer people's emotions will be in this home.

3	2	1
4	9	8
5	6	7

#3. Tree In Woman Area

A tree in this area means that those living here will be more secure and grounded in their feminine qualities. Women residing in this house will be strong-minded.

3	2	1
4	9	8
5	6	7

#9. Tree In Family Area

Be careful, if there's a tree in the family area that hangs over the house, it means all people in that house will have problems. On the other hand, if it doesn't hang over the house, everyone in this house will be independent and strong-willed.

3	2	1
4	9	8
5	6	7

CHAPTER 13
The Elements & Their Shapes

THE ANCIENT PHILOSOPHER Empedocles was the first man in Western society to categorize everything in this world, from the tiniest microbe to the stars themselves, as a construction of the four classical elements. Earth, Air, Water, and Fire.

These four can take innumerable forms, but even to this day, we are still able to categorize all physical phenomenon within the framework of the four classical elements. Our own bodies are also a construct of these same four ingredients.

Man-made structures are slightly different. Every building created utilizes five distinct building materials which are: Earth, Wood, Fire, Water, and Gold (metal). Air is purposefully not included in this list. Air is everywhere, but there isn't a particular use of air during the construction process other than manipulating and harnessing the flow of it.

Traditional Chinese Feng Shui uses five structural elements for everything including both our bodies and structures. When looking at a person's health or body, they calculate everything using the same five elements. We don't do this in this style of Feng Shui. We acknowledge a difference between our bodies and our house. Our bodies don't naturally contain wood or metal but are made in part by air. Without oxygen, every cell would die. For this reason, when looking at the body, mind, and health, we use the four classical elements. Whereas for buildings, we make use of the five structural elements.

The Five Elements Of Structure

For the purpose of this book, we will focus on the characteristics and symbols for the five structural elements. We'll introduce the basic concept of each element, then discuss each in more detail. Lastly, we'll demonstrate how the shape of your property influences your life according to the element it represents.

But first, Earth is not to be mistaken with dirt. Earth is everything in this world which has physicality. When we talk about earth as a structural element, we mean to include all solid materials, including stone or granite plus human-created materials like concrete and tile.

Wood is inevitably used in some way or another in the construction of a house. For example kitchen cabinetry, flooring, paneling, or fencing. Wood is one of the oldest and most flexible building materials used throughout history.

Fire isn't just visible flame. Fire can be a spark, glowing ember, or permeating heat. Electricity is also a form of fire. The electrical and heating systems in a building are examples of the fire element.

Water is necessary for all facets of life and used in every house. Not only is it used for construction but also daily life. Cooking, cleaning, physical nourishment, and personal hygiene, all require water. Every house uses water.

Gold is considered the epitome of metal. When referring to the five structural elements, we use the term gold when referring to any metal in a building. Metal is used in all areas of construction including frames and wiring. Metal is unique because it interacts with magnetic frequencies emitted from the earth and human-created electrical systems.

Each of these elements has its unique place in the world. They've got their own characteristics, uses, strengths, and weaknesses. For example, if you were looking for something stable, earth would be better than water. But, if you wanted something that could change and adapt quickly, earth wouldn't work.

Each of the structural elements is symbolized in a geometric shape, which we will get to in a minute. The objects around us in daily life are imbued with certain characteristics depending on the elements their shape represent. This influences our interactions with the things around us, from everyday objects we use to the houses we live in.

Over the coming pages, we'll share each element's shape and characteristics. From this, you can gain a greater understanding of your interactions with any object in your life and learn how to use this to your benefit.

Earth

Consider the characteristics associated with earth. Words such as "stable" or "unchanging" are likely to come to mind. Earth is predominantly a stable element. At a fundamental level, earth doesn't change (in comparison to other elements). The upside is we can depend on Earth's stability. Earth doesn't need any support. Its needs are simple in the world of elements.

Earth's drawback is that, if you want something to change, Earth can't help you. Earth is stubborn and set in its ways. It requires a long time and lots of effort for any change to occur.

Symbolic Shape: Square

The geometric representation of earth is the square. Similar to its element, a square is balanced, stable, and never-changing. The wind's direction changes every four months. But because of its symmetry, if the wind were to interact with a square, the result would be the same, no matter what the wind's direction was.

Square symbolizes

- Earth • Stability • Stubbornness • Conformity • Tradition •Independence.

Wood

Wood starts its life cycle as a living organism. It moves, breathes, and grows over time. Trees are adaptive to their environment. No one tree is the same. We see wood as a stable, while somewhat flexible which changes and grows over time.

When nurtured and given the right conditions, wood can flourish, becoming strong and stable. But, without constant nourishment, it becomes sick, weak, and eventually dies. In may ways, wood is like earth. It is reliable, dependable, and durable. But, wood is also flexible and allows for change.

Symbolic Shape: Rectangle

Rectangles offer similar stability to squares. But, they're not exactly symmetrical. Change is possible and inevitable. The results gained from using rectangles also differ depending on the input (what you feed it).

Rectangle Symbolizes

- Wood •Stability • Flexibility • Gradual progress • Growth • Moderate change

Fire

Imagine fire. Some characteristics (other than hot) which may come to mind are; passionate, short-lasting, changing, etc. Fire relies on continuous access to a particular supporting fuel for its survival. Without this external source, it dies immediately. If the fuel changes, so do the characteristics of the fire. It cannot stay the same.

Fire is a unique. Its process of burning is unlike any other element. No other structural or natural element can make the other elements change like fire can. Fire is a specialist in this regard.

A good thing about fire is that it always tries to grow, to be bigger and stronger, similar to human ambition. But this is also the fire's weakness. There's no solidity to it. Fire has to keep burning and using its fuel, or it will perish.

SYMBOLIC SHAPE: TRIANGLE

A triangle naturally gathers heat. If you were to place three brick walls in the shape of a triangle, no air would flow in the middle. Each of its angles would cut off the airflow.

TRIANGLE SYMBOLIZES

• Fire • Specialism • Uniqueness • Constant effort • High maintenance • Pressure

Water

In the past, water meant wealth. Only those who had water were able to grow plants, feed animals and care for others. Even to this day, water is associated with wealth and vigor. In many cultures, water is considered an element of healing, charm, and beauty too.

The fundamental characteristics we may attribute to this element include fluidity and adaptability. By nature, it's not a stable element. Water is tricky too, always finding a way to reach where it wants to go, no matter the obstacle. Nothing seeps through the cracks like water can.

A good thing about water is its ability to mix with its environment, and how it adapts according to its surroundings. The downside is that water can't be controlled, only guided.

Symbolic Shape: Polygon (5+ Angles)

Anything with five or more angles represents water. Water is both form and formless. It can take most any form. It looks different from every angle.

Polygon (5+Angles) Symbolizes

- Water • Change • Fluidity • Uncontrollable • Variability

Gold (Metal)

 Gold represents all types of metal, which is why we use the term "gold" in regards to the elements. Gold is in itself, worthless. You cannot eat it. It doesn't give you shelter. But it acts as a conduit, transferring value or energy from one place to another. Of all the elements, gold (metal) is the easiest to control, it's the one element we can shape and use in whatever way we desire.

The bad thing about gold is that its value and stability depend on whatever you mix with it. Gold isn't ever just gold. It has to have some "impurities" or other elements mixed with it. How good or bad gold is, depends on external sources and the environment it mixes with.

Symbolic Shape: Circle

Circles have no enemies. They can mix with anything and anyone. It's conducive to harnessing wind flow. But to sustain motion there has to be a continuous external source.

Circle Symbolizes

• Gold • No Enemies • Influence •Mix with anything • A Need for others.

Land & Elements

With our understanding of the structural elements and their corresponding shapes, we are able to see how the form of a building or the land on which it sits influences those living or working there.

Every plot of land on which people live or work is either allocated by the government or privately subdivided. Each plot has its own particular shape and therefore corresponding elemental influence.

Most parcels of land are rectangular in shape, but they come in all shapes. For example, it's not uncommon to see a plot of land shaped like a square, triangular, prism, or trapezoid. In this section, we'll look at the three most common land shapes and their meaning for those living within their boundaries.

SQUARE (EARTH)

As you know, squares are symbolic representations of the earth element. If a plot of land, or structure, is square-shaped, it means that those living here will have stable lives*. We can generally say that people living or working here will experience little to no change over the years. If they're poor, they'll stay poor. If they're rich, they'll stay rich. Life won't change.

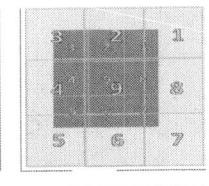

A good thing about square property plots is that, if the inhabitants' lives are already the way they want them to be, it can't get worse while living there. On the same note, if life is bad, it won't better living here either.

*Note: *The exact details of their life will depend highly on the property's address, the day of the week the inhabitants were born, and the colors they've used in their home. But these are topics for more advanced books.*

Rectangle (Wood)

Most properties are some variation of a rectangle. They may be long and narrow or short and wide. But it doesn't matter how wide or narrow the rectangle is, they all represent wood.

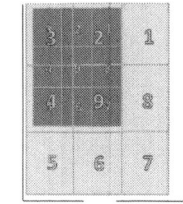

They're symbolically associated with wood, which as you know means stable but flexible with the chance to grow. From this, we can tell that anyone living on this property will have a relatively stable life, but that it will require constant effort to maintain this stability. Without their continual input and effort, their lives are able to deteriorate. Similar to how a tree needs multiple inputs to retain its vigor.

Change is certainly possible for the people living here but it takes time, and progress is slow. These people don't like to change too much too quickly. Also, because it's wood, for they will need a lot of favorable factors in their lives to see improvement, it won't be easy.

Triangle (Fire)

Often times you will see triangle shaped properties on corners or intersections. This property shape symbolizes fire. As you know, this is an element that needs regular fuel to

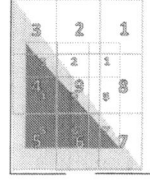

maintain itself and whose product depends on the fuel provided to it. When a flame is focused with a high-energy fuel, its intensity and power will also grow.

But what does this mean for those living on this land? A good thing about this shape is that it can make the inhabitant successful and prosperous. But, it'll only happen if they do something that requires their unique highly specialized skills or knowledge.

It's the owner's own uniqueness which fuels the fire allowing them to prosper and become wealthy. Because they're the fuel, whatever their success is cannot be passed down to the next generation or achieved without that particular individual. The next person will have to be unique in their own way. Becoming successful in something different from the last.

If a company is on this property, it will be best for them to do some kind of specialized work, with uniquely skilled employees who are specialists in their field.

CHAPTER 14
Symmetry

Balance and Communication

SYMMETRY IS ACHIEVED WHEN something is equally balanced. It is found everywhere in nature and is part of the dichotomy of life. Symmetrical balance provides the greatest results. Take for example a marble. If you were to blow air directly at the marble on a flat surface, it would (should) travel in a straight line no matter from which angle you blow. But, if the marble were smaller on one side, it would move in a curved line and change direction depending on the angle from which you blew.

This is similar to air flow around a house. Every three months, the wind's direction will change. If a house is symmetrical, it doesn't matter what time of the year it is. The wind will curve around the house, move through the house, and exit the house in a balanced manner, at any time of the year.

However, if a building is non-symmetrical, airflow may be cut off to areas during certain times of the year. Or other areas may be too windy during certain months. It won't be balanced. At this level, symmetry can mean the difference between having year-long comfort and good health or having seasonally varying health and emotional swings.

On a micro-level, symmetry plays an equally, if not more important role. We know that different areas of a property each represent an aspect of masculinity or femininity, youth, and adulthood. At this level, symmetry relates to the balance of these forces. When in balance, these forces complement one another's strengths and offset each other's weakness. However, when any one is absent, problems arise due to the imbalance.

Areas of influence can be missing for different reasons. Some plot shapes are missing particular areas due to how the land was divided. Sunken swimming pools indicate that there is literally less surface land area. Structures may also be designed in ways where an area is missing. For example, if the house is an L shape.

In this chapter, we'll take a look at examples of common asymmetrical structure and land shapes, plus their meanings (and problem) for those living there.

Angle Shapes

Houses come in many shapes and forms. One typical example is the angle shaped house. Angle shapes are characterized by "missing" an area from what would otherwise make them a square or rectangle. The next few pages will provide examples of angle-shaped properties, and their meanings. The meanings are the same whether it's the land or the structure which is in this shape. Keep in mind that all the images are from a bird's eye view perspective.

Missing Man Area

Here the right back area is missing from the land's geometric shape as seen from a bird's eye view. Looking from the road, this structure wouldn't have a roof or structure in the far right area, at the back of the property. This is interpreted as a weakness in the Man's zone. Correspondingly, any man living in the house would act more childlike. It also means that the woman living in this house is more dominant than the man.

Missing Woman Area

Where the woman's area is missing from the land or structure, we can see that a woman living here wouldn't be "archetypically feminine."

For example, she may not be very detail-oriented, or emotionally driven. Instead, she'd likely be task-oriented, ambitious and tough on the outside.

Missing Boy Area

When the land or building is lacking a child's area, and a woman there falls pregnant, it is almost impossible that the child will be the gender that is missing.

In this example, the boy's area is missing. A child born here would likely be a girl. A man in this house tends to be sober and less playful, due to the missing boy influence. Any males' own boy-like characteristics are also less prominent.

Missing Girl Area

In this case, it's the young girl are which is missing from the structure or land. Like the boy's example, this will influence the pregnancy of any woman living here.  They'd be much more likely to give birth to a boy rather than a girl. Women living here are also more likely to express stronger adult feminine characteristics than childlike ones. Women are likely organized and critical of their surroundings and those close to them. They could almost be considered a serious mothering type.

Horseshoe Shapes

Another common form is the horseshoe. If we looked at the property from above, it would look similar to a horseshoe or "U" shape. This indicates a rift in communication between the two areas separated by the gap. This form is especially influential on couples and families. In the worst-case scenario, it can lead to divorce.

BACK-FACING HORSESHOE

A back-facing horseshoe is where the Adult 3rd-Sex area is missing. This reveals a lack of communication between the adult men and women living here. If a couple lives here, they'll have communication issues, or simply won't talk much with each other when at home.

FRONT-FACING HORSESHOE

A front-facing horseshoe is where the Young 3rd-Sex is missing. If young children live in the house together, they won't be close to those of the opposite sex. For example, if a family lives here including a daughter and son, the two kids will have their own lives, and wouldn't be interested in spending time with each other.

Side-Facing Horseshoe

Structures missing an area either on the left or the right side of the structure (or land), represents a separation between parents and their children.

If the Teenage Girl Area is missing, it means that, although they would love each other, a mother and her daughter wouldn't talk much with each other. In contrast, if the Teenage Boy Area is missing, the same scenario would exist between the father and the son. They wouldn't talk with each other that often, or at least won't speak in depth about their lives with each other.

CHAPTER 15
Summary & Index

Practice Deepens Understanding

WE'VE COVERED SO MUCH, but there still so much more. We could have touched on colors, numbers or weekday astrology, which all connect to Feng Shui. But we chose not to because it's more valuable to first understand the fundamental 9 areas and their influences before confusing yourself with other variables. The 9 areas of influence already give you so many tools to take control of your life and the ability to help others do the same. This chapter allows you to quickly review the essential aspects of each area and its meaning in connections to the different rooms of an average house.

The 9 Areas

Every property can be segmented into 9 areas of influence. Divide your land, as seen from above, into a tic tac toe board. The main road will be at the bottom of the grid, and back of the property at the top. The #1. area, will be at the back right, #2 at the back middle and so on. Each represents a masculine/feminine, child/adult force which influences our everyday behavior, habits, and thoughts. Here are the key characteristics of each area:

3. Woman area	2. Adult 3rd-Sex area	1. Man area
- Organized - Detail Oriented - Care taker - Intimate/romantic - Image is everything - Responsibility - Plans ahead - Constantly active	- Emotional - Does everything according to mood - Highly creative Thinks different - Private - Duck	- Unorganized - Big/Grandiose - Focused - Sensual - Ambitious - Straight to the point - Spontaneous - Flashy
4. Teenage girl area	**9. Family area**	**8. Teenage boy area**
- Private - Routine - Image-focused - Gossips - Organized - Uncreative - Good memory - Active out of house	- Never acts alone - Always helping or being helped - Only 1 real leader - Either many people or nobody - Problems but can fix	- Trendy - Does to look good - Social - Loves new technology - Insecure - Great talker - Competitive
5. Young girl area	**6. Young 3rd-Sex**	**7. Young Boy area**
- Creative - Dreamer - Perfectionist - Bossy - Cannot sit still - Loves attention - Acts from emotions	- Quiet - Very private - Indecisive - Misunderstood - Has their own world - Withdrawn - Thinks a lot - Short-tempered	- Social - Looks for new things - Very active - Not honest with themselves - Never thinks ahead - Often in debt

The Bedroom

The bedroom reveals the personality of whoever sleeps in that room. The location of the bedroom shows us how a person behaves in the house and their relationships with others. We're able to know their sex life too. Here's a what the location of your bedroom says about your personality and sex style:

3. Bedroom - Detail-oriented - Nags a lot - Plans a head - Motherly - All about appearances *Sex: Routine & Romance*	**2. Bedroom** - Emotional swings - Don't like change - Thinks a lot - Everything by mood - Highly creative - Indecisive *Sex: When in the mood*	**1. Bedroom** - Stays at home a lot - Comfort first - Logical thinker - Quick thinker and decision maker - Single-minded. *Sex: Duty, adventurous*
4. Bedroom - Private at home - Clean but messy - Good at routine - Insecure - Blames others - Lacks self-insight *Sex: Insecure. Others do.*	**9. Bedroom** - Knows everything that happens in the house - Involved in everyone's business - If strong will command everyone. If weak, everyone will	**8. Bedroom** - Likes excitement - Hates routine - Loves up to date things - Playful - Social - Wants to show off - Never cleans
5. Bedroom - Attention-seekers - Doesn't sleep much - Dreamer - All about emotions - Doesn't like being alone *Sex: snuggle & attention.*	**6. Bedroom** - Goes unnoticed - Thinks differently - Feels unappreciated - Restless sleeper - Worries a lot - Never praised for what they do *Sex: Only because of*	**7. Bedroom** - Hates routine - Playful & Messy - Don't sleep a lot - Don't think about others. - Loves to be active *Sex: Beware, bored easy.*

The Toilet/Bathroom

The toilet represents how we spend money. It reveals how a person makes money decisions, and what they actually spend their money on. It also shows their general behavior when using the bathroom. Here is what your toilet says about your spending habits depending on its location on the property:

3. Toilet	2. Toilet	1. Toilet
- Buys "Sales". - Lots of small things - Spends money on other people - Likes knickknacks. *Bathroom is immaculate.*	- Uses money - others don't understand - Indecisive - Buys what makes them feel good. *Lots of time in the bathroom. No-one knows what they do.*	- Spends big amounts. - Buys new and best quality. - Likes to show off what they buy. *Likes to spend a lot of time in the bathroom.*
4. Toilet	**9. Toilet**	**8. Toilet**
- Buys trendy things - Emotional shopper. - Never shops alone. - Has to have what friends have. *Never tidy but everything in its place.*	- Always spend on others/family - Whenever have - spend it straight away. - Buying habits always changing. *Toilet used often by everyone. Messy.*	- Buys things to impress others. - Loves technology - Spends on fun & entertainment. *Tidy but not clean.*
5. Toilet	**6. Toilet**	**7. Toilet**
- Buys little things. - Don't think before - Loves to buy for the experience. - Buys to make them feel special. *Untidy. In & out.*	- Buys things others wouldn't think of. - Only spends on self. - Private with money. - Indecisive spenders *Toilet doesn't get used much, or cleaned.*	- Spends more than they have (in debt) - Spontaneous shop - Bored quickly with what they buy. *In and out. Careless.*

Kitchen

The kitchen is where everyone in the house come together. Especially in the context of a family. It reveals the relationships dynamics between everyone living in the house. This room also represents people's cooking styles and dining behaviors. Here's what your kitchen's location says about you:

3. Kitchen	2. Kitchen	1. Kitchen
- Like to eat routine. - Proper dinner every night & manners. - Eats everything for reason. *Formal dinners in this area. Good manners!*	- People have own routines - Won't eat together every night.. *When sit together, won't talk, or small talk.*	- Family is close - Like big dinners - Don't eat at the same time every night but eat together. - Cooks lots of things *Loud and fun at the dinner table. Chatty.*
4. Kitchen - Like keeping to themselves at home. - Used every day. - Stick to routine food they know. *No dinner guests. Private*	**9. Kitchen** - Love time together. - Rare to be alone. - Lots of arguments but resolved. *Kitchen only used if a big group are eating together.*	**8. Kitchen** - Straight forward talkers - Have guests often - Loves new things. - Will try anything, *Everyone talks a lot but not about self.*
5. Kitchen - Don't talk much - Everyone has their own lives *Kitchen only gets used to make coffee or heat food. Not often used for cooking.*	**6. Kitchen** - Only argue or talk about things that are wrong. - Won't spend time together in the house. *Kitchen not used for cooking.*	**7. Kitchen** - Fun, talkative. - Talks about themselves - Looks good = lacks flavor. Looks bad, = taste good. *Often breaks things in the kitchen. Tries new*

Living Room

The living room symbolizes a person's social life. It reveals how people act with their friends, and if they invite people to their homes often. Here's what your living room says about you dependant on where is it in the house:

3. Living Room	2. Living Room	1. Living Room
- Appearance is everything. - Everything has its own special place. - Only invite important people. *Mostly small talk only.*	- Don't like to entertain people. - Only talk to people like them. - Never talks about problems. *Won't feel relaxed here.*	- Love to entertain. - Have friends over. - Comfort #1 - Like showing off to friends. Big TVs etc. *When with friends will be loud and high energy.*
4. Living Room - Like small circles of friends. - Only invite trusted people to their house *Will always clean up before having people over because they're messy.*	**9. Living Room** - Never used by just one person. - If only 1 person lives in the house, will never use it - Always have family come over to visit.	**8. Living Room** - Love spending time with friends. - Relaxed atmosphere. — Self service - Likely untidy room. *Will often have people over to their home. Fun and social times.*
5. Living Room - Have a hard time trusting people - Keeps their home life and outside life separate. *Won't use this living room often.*	**6. Living Room** - People living here are very private. - The room won't be used often. *This room will usually be used by only one person each time. If more they won't talk.*	**7. Living Room** - Don't sit and relax. - Have active social lives, but not at home. *If have friends over, will only be there a short time. If friends stay longer, will go into a different room.*

Office

A workspace corresponds to a person's work style and behavior when working. This applies for both a private workspace at home and where one sits at the office. Here's what the location of your desk or workstation says about your work style:

3. Office	2. Office	1. Office
- Multi-tasking. - Always double checks their work. Focused on detail. - Good at delegating - Works in structure. - Everything planned.	- Highly creative. Great for new ideas. - Loves recognition. - Hate routine work. - Never listen to others - Jack of all trades	- Sit for long periods - Highly focused - Want perfect, but makes little mistakes - Big picture thinkers. - Focused on results. Do everything by themselves.
4. Office	**9. Office**	**8. Office**
- Good with routine. - Good for papers. - Not creative. - Not team players, like to work alone. - If it isn't their duty, they won't do it.	- Always helps others with problems - If single office will be used for storage. - Good for meetings or communal space for people to come together.	- Good with competitive tasks - Good for sales. - Everything up to date. - Hates paperwork & routine work.
5. Office	**6. Office**	**7. Office**
- Thinks what they do is important. - Want recognition - Quality of work depends on mood. - Great at improving appearances.	- Cannot be a leader. - What they think is good, others don't. - Good for routine and structured work. - If not kept busy, will not take initiative themselves.	- Get bored easily. - Don't sit behind their desks for long - Love new /change. -Tendency not to finish projects - Good customer service.

CHAPTER 16
Readings By Aur

It's time to bring it all together. We've gathered a few floor plans to use as examples so you how Aur herself analyzes a house using the 9 areas of influence and other factors we've covered.

Each of the floor plans is an actual student's home. Aur has looked at each one and shared her analysis of the people's lives. Try to understand how she comes to her conclusions using what you've learned from this book. Let's get started.

Sample House 1. Jenny's (Name Changed) Townhouse.

Jenny, a professional 30+-year-old woman, works in advertising. She lives on her own in a two-story home in Australia.

Aur's Analysis

Let's first look at Jenny's personality. You can see that most of the building falls within the boundaries of the male area. This means that anyone living here will seem harsh and straight to the point, like a man.

However, as you can see (on the next page) her bedroom is in the Woman's Area of the house. This means that although she seems tough like a man on the outside, she's actually soft and quite feminine in private. Most people wouldn't know this about her, though. Also, because the bedroom is located in the Woman's Area, we can tell that Jenny is a proud and confident person. But she's also a perfectionist, and never feels like her home is perfect, yet. She always feels that she can add something to improve it or make it more beautiful.

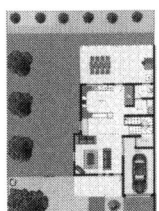

If we look carefully, we see that Jenny's bedroom is actually slightly in the Adult 3rd-Sex Area of the land too. This reveals that it takes a lot for Jenny to like something. It's not easy for her to be impressed or fall in love with something. This will be true for her relationships too. It'll be difficult for her to find someone she finds attractive.

Although people wouldn't expect it of her (because the house is on the male side), Jenny does love romance and intimacy. This is evident from her bedroom being in the

Woman zone. However, when she is in a relationship, she will want to keep it private.

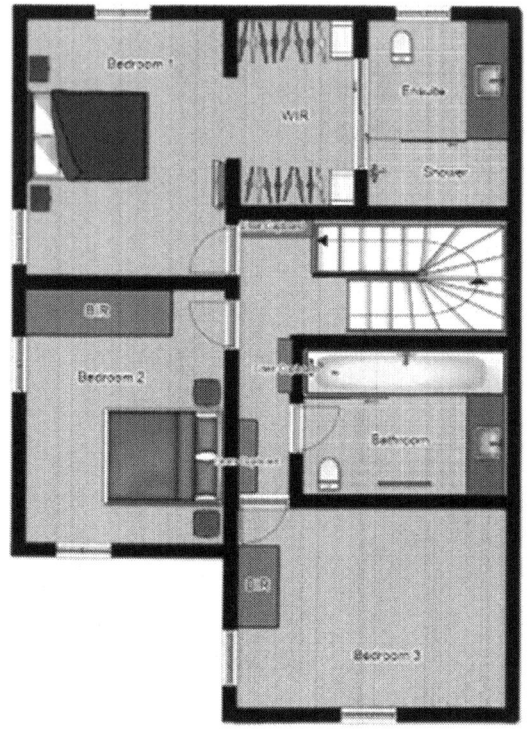

The upstairs area

This is because of the 3rd-Sex influence on the bedroom. It reflects how 3rd-gender personalities like to keep aspects of their life private. Jenny won't want other people to know about her private relationships, especially her family.

Next, if we look at the bathroom closest to her room, we see that, when Jenny wants to buy something, she won't worry about the price tag. This is because her toilet is the Man Area of the house, opposite her bedroom. Another thing we notice is that her toilet is perpendicular to the road. This means that she'll spend a lot of money each month. But, because Jenny makes her own money, she feels like she can spend it however she likes.

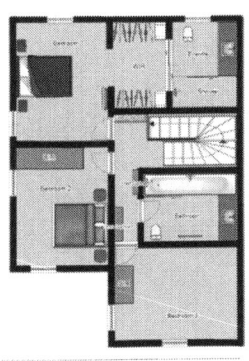

Let's connect what we know about Jenny and her spending habits with the fact that it's difficult for her to find things she likes. This shows that when Jenny does finally see something that she fancies, she'll buy it without worrying about its price. Jenny also likes to spend her money on big items. You can ee this from the toilet being in the Man Area. Most women usually like to shop a lot and buy many things, especially when they're on sale, but not Jenny.

If Jenny would like to spend less money each month, we could help her by suggesting to place a U-shaped carpet under her toilet. This would counter the perpendicularity problem.

We can see that the living room is in between the Young Girl and Teenage Girl Areas of the building. This reveals that Jenny won't invite people over, even though she's proud of her home. Jenny will only allow people to come over if she trusts them a lot and has known them for a long time.

Those around Jenny think she is friendly and easy-going, but in truth, she's private and likes to keep her home life separate from the rest of her life.

Lastly, Jenny's kitchen is the Woman Area of the house but is also in the Family Area of the entire property. You can see that although she loves to cook, she won't do it very often because she lives alone.

On the rare occasion she does decide to cook, she'll make sure everything is perfect and beautifully presented. When most people buy a sandwich or take away food, they won't care about how it looks. They'll eat straight from the box. But not Jenny. She'll serve herself on a plate and eat properly, no matter what she's eating.

Sample House 2. The Wong (Name Changed) Family Home

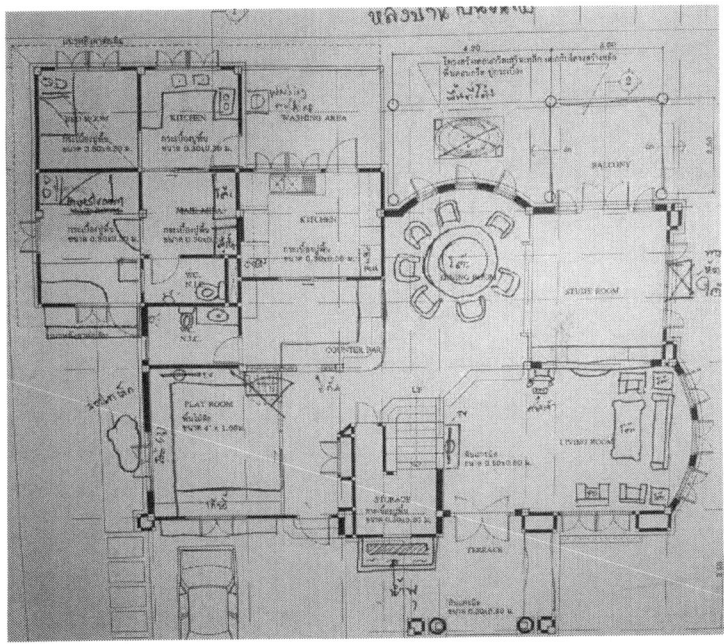

The Wong family are a wealthy family of Chinese descent who own their own business and live in Bangkok, Thailand. We'll focus on the ground floor for this example.

Aur's Analysis

First of all, if we would like to see how a family communicates with each other, a good place to start is dining room table. The Wong family's floorplan shows us that their dining room table is positioned primarily in the Family Area and that the kitchen is in the Adult 3rd-Sex Area.

This shows us that the table won't often be used, only when there are lots of people. Additionally, the table is directly in the path of the front door. Whenever you see a table like this, you can tell that the people sitting here will argue a lot. This is because when a front door is directly facing a table, the wind will hit it straight on. The wind brings both everything good and bad with it. In this case, it is bringing everything right to that table.

This analysis is confirmed by the table's position. It's close to the Family Area, so you already know that the Wong family will quarrel often. This is exaggerated more because the table itself is round which represents gold. Gold is always influenced by its surroundings and isn't stable in of itself. So, at a round table, each person will bring their own opinion, but no one person will be able to act as the single "head of the table" to control the situation.

People may suggest that it's right for all people to be equal. However, relationships between any social animals involve hierarchy. This is natural. It creates balance and order. The problem is, everyone at this table will be confident. They won't conform to a family hierarchy. The children will be argumentative and stubborn, which also goes against Chinese culture.

In general, round tables can be good in situations which require brainstorming or delegation, as long as you allow the others to do things their own way. This is why many new startups, technology, or creative companies work very well when they have round tables. In those cases, each person in the meeting is usually a specialist with a valuable and unique opinion. The management system is also less hierarchal in many new companies.

When taking a further look at the Wong Family's home, we see that the maid's quarters are at the back of the house. This reveals that she has likely been with the family for a long time. Her room is in a position of high power. The owner's bedroom (not shown here), is upstairs and is closer to the front of the house. This means that they won't be able to command the maid like a child cannot command an adult. In the case of the Wong family, it's likely that the owner wouldn't spend much time at home, and that they'd leave the maid in charge of the house.

Another sign that the Wong family wouldn't spend much time at home is because of where they park their car. We know that nothing in the children's areas can stay there for long periods of time. So, when a car is parked in front of a property, it means that the owner is usually not home. The Wong's car is parked in the young girl position, meaning that they will have to leave the house often. Most modern homes park their cars at the front, which corresponds with the busy modern lifestyle where we spend most of our time away from home. This is often different for an older person or a wealthy individual's home. Many have cars in the back of the property, meaning that they spend much of their time at home.

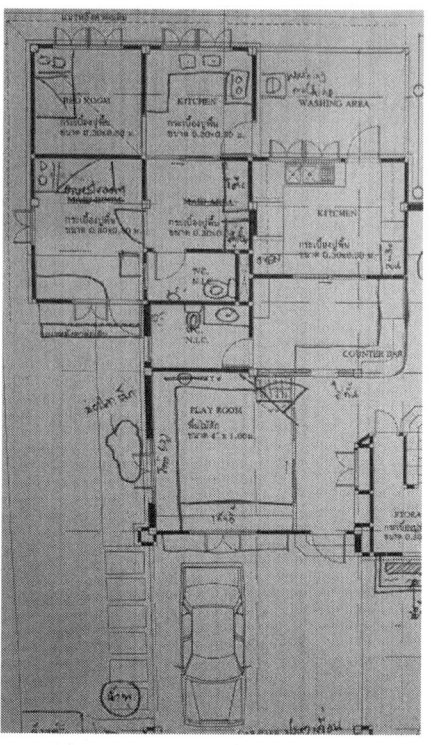

Lastly, the Wong's toilet reveals that the Wong family cares a lot about how they look in their social circles. Their guest bathroom is on the woman's side of the house, in the Teenage Girl Area, and perpendicular to the road. This means that the Wong family likes to spend a lot of money to make themselves look good. This is similar to how most teenage girls see their appearance and social standing as paramount and spend a lot of money keeping up appearances.

Sample House 3. Debbie (Name Changed) And Her Husband

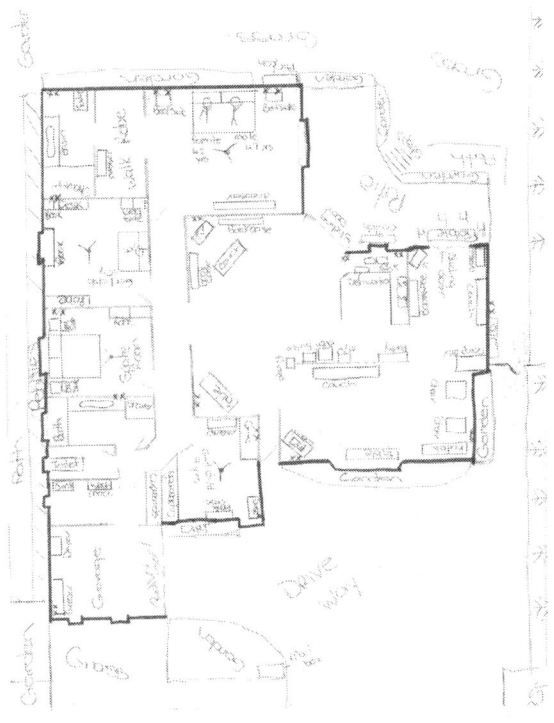

Debbie is a stay-at-home mom and lives with her husband Tom in a one-story home in Australia. They live with their two children.

Aur's Analysis

Let's start with the bedroom, which is in the 3-rd Sex Area. We're are able to see that Tom will be stubborn but won't show that he is. When you ask him to do something, he won't say no. But, he won't do it either. The more you nag at someone like Tom, the quieter he'll become. When he does talk, he'll often say things you would never have expected to hear. Debbie and Tom's sex life wouldn't be exciting. When one is in the mood, the other won't be, and vice versa. As we know, it's difficult for a couple to have a healthy love life if sleeping in this area. The position of the bedroom also reveals that Tom doesn't typically show appreciation or affection for his wife while at home either. He won't know how Debbie feels and won't know how to be close to her. But, the location of their bed shows that they'll feel it's normal. They won't see it as a big problem.

Lastly, let's look at the bathroom. Their toilet reveals that they're always buying little things for the house and mostly for other people, rather than themselves. This is because it's in the Woman Area and perpendicular to the road. The shower is in the Young Girl Area of that room. This indicates that Debbie likes to buy new shampoos and conditioners for their smells, but never finishes the old bottles before buying new ones.

The laundry is in the young girl position. Debbie and Tom don't like to do laundry often. They won't care whether their clothes are washed every day or not.

CHAPTER 17
Self-Quiz

THIS IS THE FINAL SECTION where you get the opportunity to practice your newfound skills for yourself by analyzing a person's life using Aur's Feng Shui. We've included multiple simple case studies for you to practice with. Each case study includes a floor plan and details of the people living there.

Each example has a multiple-choice questionnaire, and an open-ended question about the inhabitant's personality, relationships, and lifestyle. By now you should be able to answer each question from looking at the floor plan. Try it and check your answers in the back.

Self Quiz 1.
Amy, Ted, and Daniel

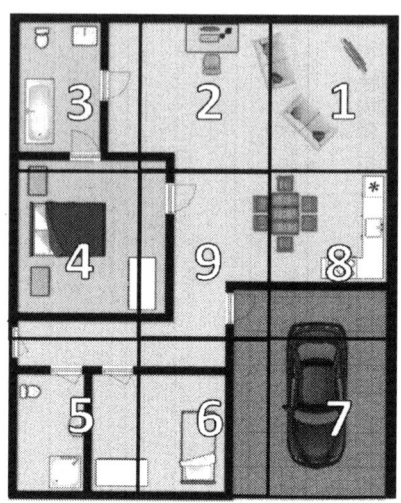

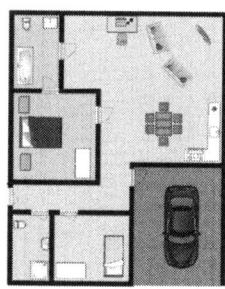

Take a look at the floor plan provided. Imagine a couple by the names of Amy and Ted live here with their son Daniel, who's 10 years old. Amy is a stay at home mom. She also works part-time from home as a bookkeeper. Ted works full-time for an insurance company. We can see that Amy and Ted's bedroom is in the teenage girl position. Amy sleeps on the left-hand side of the bed, and Ted on the right. Amy is closer to the back of the house. Daniel's bedroom is in the 3rd-sex child position. Here are some questions about their lives.

QUESTION 1.

How would you best describe Ted's personality?
- A. *Quiet at home likes routine but gets annoyed easily.*
- B. *Highly organized, detail-oriented, and stubborn.*
- C. *Thinks differently than others, restless sleeper, and worries a lot.*
- D. *Hates routine, messy, doesn't sleep a lot and gets bored quickly.*

QUESTION 2.

How would you describe Amy's spending habits?
- A. *Always spending too much money on big things*
- B. *Spends a lot of money on little things. But usually for other people*
- C. *Likes to keep up to date with new technology and trends.*
- D. *Can never make up her mind when they go shopping.*

QUESTION 3.

Amy's desk is in the Adult 3rd sex area. What could her problem be?
- A. *Amy focuses too much on the little details.*
- B. *Amy can never plan ahead for upcoming work.*
- C. *Amy cannot come up with new ideas sitting here.*
- D. *Amy uses her computer too much for socializing with others.*

QUESTION 4.

Describe this family's dining habits.

- A. *They don't often eat at home. They hardly use the kitchen.*
- B. *They like routine and have a reason for everything they eat.*
- C. *They don't usually eat together and have different habits.*
- D. *They like trying new things and will usually eat together.*

QUESTION 5.

What can you say about Amy, Ted, and Daniel's social life? Do you see any problems in their home that can be fixed? Please take a look in the back to find the answers.

Self Quiz 2.
Jeff's condo

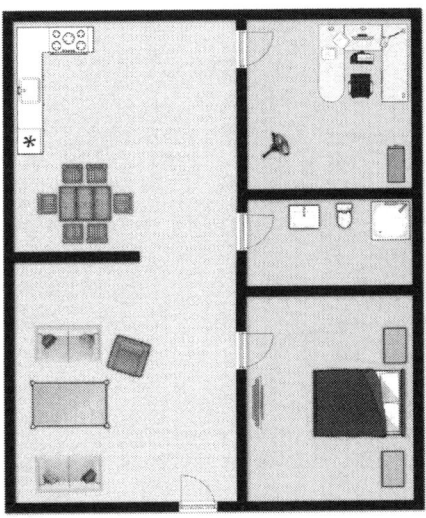

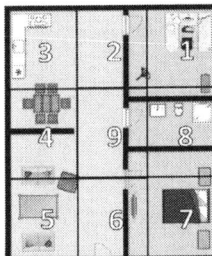

Take a look at the floor plan provided. This is Jeff's two bedroom, one bathroom condo. Jeff is an English teacher. He lives by himself with his cat, Mr. Smiggles. As you can see from the picture, Jeff's bedroom is in the Young Boy area. He uses the back bedroom as his home office. Try answering the questions below about Jeff.

QUESTION 1.

How would you describe Jeff's personality?

    A. *Jeff keeps his home life private, likes routine, gets annoyed easily.*

    B. *Hates routine, messy, doesn't sleep a lot and gets bored quickly.*

    C. *Often feels unappreciated, restless sleeper, and worries a lot.*

    D. *Highly organized, detail-oriented, in touch with his softer side.*

QUESTION 2.

How would you describe Jeff's social life at home?

    A. *Jeff loves having people over for gatherings.*

    B. *He only allows people he knows closely into his home.*

    C. *He's always having people over for laid back socializing.*

    D. *He only has people over if he thinks they're important, and always cleans beforehand.*

QUESTION 3.

How would you describe Jeff's spending habits?

    A. *Jeff likes to keep up to date with the latest trends.*

    B. *Jeff spends his money on big items and doesn't care about prices.*

    C. *Jeff enjoys buying things that make him feel good about himself.*

    D. *Jeff loves to spend his money on family, often helping financially.*

QUESTION 4.

How would you describe Jeff's eating habits?

    A. *Jeff doesn't like to eat at home. If he does, it's home delivery.*

    B. *Jeff eats at home and always likes to eat something different.*

    C. *Jeff wants routine and always eats a proper meal.*

    D. *Jeff only cooks big meals if his friends come over. Otherwise, he eats whatever is easiest.*

QUESTION 5.

What can you say about Jeff's work habits when he's at home? Do you see any problems with his house that can be fixed? Please take a look in the back to find the answers.

Self Quiz 3
Patty and Anthony

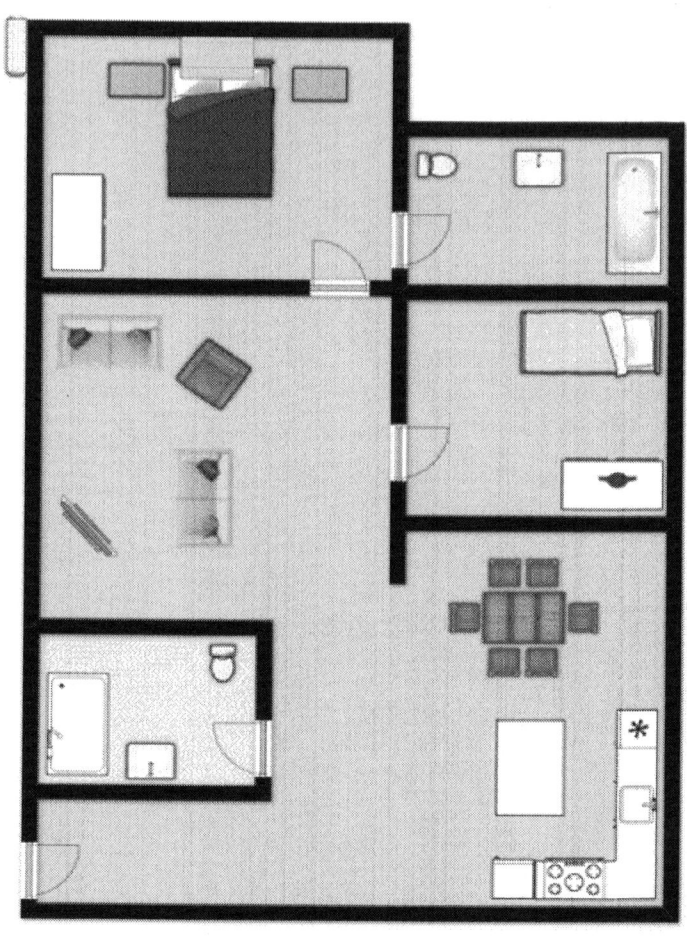

Patty and Anthony are a young couple. They live in a two-bedroom home and use the second bedroom for guests. Patty is a junior architect, and Anthony is a police officer. Anthony sleeps on the right side of the bed, closest to the toilet. Patty sleeps on the left. There is an air conditioner above their bed. Try and answer the following questions.

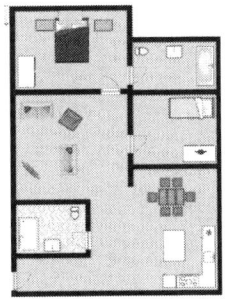

QUESTION 1.

How would you describe Patty & Anthony's sex life?

A. *Patty likes sex frequently as it makes her feel close to Anthony, but Anthony usually isn't in the mood.*

B. *Anthony enjoys sex more than Patty, and sometimes feels bored and wants to try something new.*

C. *They won't have sex often, and when they do, it's because they feel it should be done, not necessarily because they want it.*

D. *Both Anthony and Patty enjoy sex and like to be creative when together. Anthony likes to have sex depending on his mood, Patty likes to plan it.*

QUESTION 2.

What can you say about Patty & Anthony's behavior at the dinner table?

A. *Patty & Anthony like to be straight forward and casual.*

B. *They don't like to talk about themselves, keep the conversation light.*

    C. *They try to be well-mannered, even when it's just the two of them.*

    D. *They usually like a quiet dinner, and don't talk much.*

QUESTION 3.

What are Patty's spending habits like?

    A. *She isn't careful and is a spontaneous shopper. She always gets bored quickly with things she buys.*

    B. *She always looks for things on sale, and never buys just one.*

    C. *She buys anything that will make her feel special, even if it isn't useful.*

    D. *She never knows what to buy, and always buys differently than others.*

QUESTION 4.

Which of these best describes Anthony?

    A. *Loves routine, private at home, doesn't understand his feelings*

    B. *Logical and decisive, adventurous, confident and boisterous*

    C. *Indecisive, thinks a lot, everything depends on mood*

    D. *Messy, loves new things, playful, likes to be with friends*

QUESTION 5.

What can you say about Patty and Anthony's social life at home? Do you see any problems with this house that can be fixed? Take a look in the back to find the answers.

Answers - Self Quiz

Let's see how you went with the self-quiz. Here are the answers.

Self-Quiz 1
Amy, Ted, and Daniel

Q1.A Q2.B Q3.B Q4.D

Question 5.

Amy, Ted, and Daniel place high value their social life. They don't have people come over often, but when they do, it'll be a roaring fun time. When they use the living room, they'll stay there for long periods. One problem is that their toilet in the en-suite is perpendicular to the road. In this area, it means that Amy, Ted, and Daniel, will spend money on lots of little things and by the time they realize it, they will have nothing left by the end of the month. Also, because Daniel's bedhead is facing the road, he will have trouble getting deep sleep and may have problems with his brain such as frequent headaches or dullness.

Self-Quiz 2
Jeff

Q1.B Q2.B Q3.A Q4.C

QUESTION 5.

When Jeff works at home, he 'll be doing things for extended periods of time. He 'll often be so focused on what he's doing too that he'll likely lose track of time. It's possible that Jeff will have lower back and knee problems, because of the TV at the foot of his bed. This will affect the nerves in his legs and lower back. Also, it will be very hard for Jeff to save money because his toilet is facing towards the road.

SELF-QUIZ 3.
PATTY AND ANTHONY

Q1.D Q2.A Q3.D Q4.C

QUESTION 5.

Patty and Anthony don't often have friends over to their house. They like to keep their home life and social life separate. When they do have friends over it will usually be only in small groups and only people they have known for a long time. The most pressing problem is the air-conditioning unit above their bed. This will adversely affect Patty & Anthony's health. They'll be sick often and likely feel groggy or have headaches frequently. In the worst-case long-term scenario, this could lead to dementia or other brain problems.

Thank you

About Aur

- Consultant for over $5 Billion in property.
- Private advisor to 200+ of Asia's most influential people *(Heads of State, Forbes 100)*
- TV Host for 9 years on self-titled Feng Shui Show in Thailand.

Bangkok-based Aur consults, lectures and presents on a style of Feng Shui unique to herself and an ancient personality profiling system, based on the classical elements she calls Taksa.

In short: she 'reads' people and houses, helping individuals through personal or business challenges by giving them the tools using their natural surroundings and connection to nature.

Aur has hosted various television shows which at their peak attracted millions of Thai viewers. Nowadays, Aur spends most of her time mentoring students both offline and online. She teaches workshops, seminars and performs guest speeches around the World.

Made in the USA
San Bernardino, CA
05 August 2018